My Dog Knows It's Sunday

My Dog Knows It's Sunday

... And 30 Other Bible-Based Meditations

Series # 8

Roger Ellsworth

Unless otherwise noted, Scripture quotations are taken from the New King James Version®. Copyright © 1982 by Thomas Nelson. Used by permission. All rights reserved.

Copyright © 2018, Roger Ellsworth

All rights reserved. No part of this book may be reproduced, scanned, or distributed in any printed or electronic form without permission.

First Edition: 2018

ISBN: 978-0-9996559-6-2

20180825LSI

Great Writing Publications
www.greatwriting.org
Taylors, SC

www.greatwriting.org

Purpose

My Coffee Cup Meditations are short, easy-to-read, engagingly presented devotions based on the Bible, the Word of God. Each reading takes a single idea or theme and develops it in a thought-provoking way so that you are inspired to consider the greatness of God, the relevance of the good news of the life, death, resurrection, and coming-again of Jesus, and are better equipped for life in this world and well prepared for the world to come.

www.mycoffeecupmeditations.com

https://www.facebook.com/MyCoffeeCupMeditations/

Dedication

To

The members of
Mary's Chapel Baptist Church,
Ripley, TN

About This Book

This book is the result of the labors Roger Ellsworth and the thought he has given to various passages of Scripture over the years. You may read more about Roger on page 141.

We hope you will enjoy these Bible-based meditations. We would love to hear from you, so please send us a note to tell us what you think—which ones you liked most, and how they made a difference in your life or in the life of a family member, friend, or work associate. To reach us online, go to www.mycoffeecupmeditations.com/contact

Table of Contents

1 My Dog Knows It's Sunday 16
2 "He Never Woke Anybody Up" 20
3 "The Word of the LORD came" 24
4 Why Believe the Bible? 28
5 How the Word of God Comes to Us (1) 32
6 How the Word of God Comes to Us (2) 36
7 Races and Runners 40
8 Why Jonah Ran 44
9 Backsliding 48
10 Watch! 52
11 Storms and Sleepers 56
12 The Captain and the Crew 60
13 One Big Gulp 64
14 Jonah's Revival 68
15 Experiencing Revival 72
16 The Resurrection of Jesus 76
17 Re-sending, Repenting, and Relenting 80
18 Jonah's Message and Ours 84
19 The Pitiful Prophet Who Couldn't Pity 88
20 The Compassion of Jesus 92
21 Chastisement 96
22 Where's the Mumbo? Where's the Jumbo? 100
23 The Man Who Got His Bible Back 104
24 A Hymn's Question Answered 108
25 The Message of Heaven in the Mockery of Hell 112

26 Easter: Amazing, But Not Surprising 116
27 A Psalm for Cave Dwellers.. 120
28 Mistaken Assumptions.. 124
29 My Heavenly Father Watches Over Me.................................. 128
30 Blessed Assurance 132
31 Liar and Truth-Teller 136

About the Author 141
The Series 142

The App

www.mycoffeecupmeditations.com

Be sure you get the app!

-1-

From God's Word, the Bible...

Now on the first day of the week, when the disciples came together to break bread, Paul, ready to depart the next day, spoke to them and continued his message until midnight.

Acts 20:7

My Dog Knows It's Sunday

I don't know how my dog Molly knows, but she knows. She knows when Sunday arrives. I've tried to figure out how she knows, and I keep coming up empty. But from the very time she gets up on Sunday, she seems to act differently than on other days. Early on Sunday mornings, I place my Bible on the small table by the garage door. But Molly always senses its Sunday before I do that. Before my wife and I start getting dressed for church, Molly knows its Sunday. Maybe it's the hymns. Sylvia and I always listen to hymns as we get ready for church. But Molly seems to know its Sunday before we crank up the hymns. I wonder what her clue is.

Whatever it is, Molly knows its Sunday, and she knows Sunday is different than the other days of the week. It's special. Do we know as much as Molly? Do we know that Sunday is special?

I've seen many changes among God's people over the

years. One of the biggest is their attitude toward Sunday. When I was growing up it was commonly believed that God's people should treat Sunday as a day of rest from the things that occupy us the rest of the week. It was regarded as a day for public worship and a day to minister to others.

But many no longer believe that. They believe that there are only nine commandments, not ten. They insist that the Sabbath day commandment no longer applies. They look upon it as something that pertained only to the Jews in the Old Testament era.

It's true, of course, that we no longer observe the Sabbath on Saturday, as the Jews did. The resurrection of Christ was an event of such monumental significance that it changed the day of worship from the seventh day to the first. We can see that change in the life of the early church (Acts 20:7; 1 Cor. 16:2), which apparently made it because the Lord revealed that they should do so.

But the change from the seventh day to the first day doesn't mean that we should treat the day as if it were like all the other days.

Many no longer have a Lord's Day. They have a Lord's Hour, or maybe two hours. We've reached the point where it's acceptable to go to church for an hour on Sunday morning (if it's convenient and there's nothing else we want to do), and then go back to life as usual.

Churches used to encourage people to give the whole of the Lord's Day to the Lord by having both morning and evening worship services, but that practice is largely gone. Church leaders blame church members for the loss of Sunday evening services. They tell us that they had to stop them because the people wouldn't attend. And church members blame church leaders for not giving the Sunday evening services the effort that they deserved.

Several years ago, a lady confronted me in a rather blustery way: "Preacher, we don't have to go to church on Sunday evening. The Bible doesn't command it."

My response was this: "Why don't we want to?" Even if God hadn't commanded us to set apart one day to worship and praise Him, I should think that we would have thought of it ourselves.

What kind of Christianity is it that makes us want to do just as little as we can? What kind of Christianity is it that makes us want to minimize?

I'm happy that the Lord Jesus didn't take the minimal approach to saving us. I'm glad He didn't say to the Father: "Yes, I will go to Bethlehem, but I will not go to Calvary. I will go to earth to show them that You love them, to show them how to live and to teach them Your ways, but I will not die for them. I will not take the wrath that they deserve for their sins."

A minimal Christ doing the minimum for us would never have saved us. Why do we want to do so little for Him when He has done so much for us?

Molly doesn't know much about Sunday except that it's a special day. We who know so much more than she should go out of our way to make it, not just another day, but a special day.

-2-

From God's Word, the Bible...

And do this, knowing the time, that now it is high time to awake
out of sleep; for now our salvation is nearer
than when we first believed.

Therefore He says:
"Awake, you who sleep,
Arise from the dead,
And Christ will give you light."

Romans 13:11; Ephesians 5:14

"He Never Woke Anybody Up"

A woman was speaking about her pastor who had recently left to serve another church. She had very kind and positive things to say. "He was a very nice man," she said. "We really loved him," she said. To those statements she added two or three more compliments. It was obvious that she held him in high esteem.

Then she said something rather startling: "But he never woke anybody up."

Those words prompted me to do some soul-searching about my own preaching. Am I waking anybody up?

Sinners need to be awakened. That's for sure. One of our old hymns describes those apart from Christ as "slumbering on the brink of woe."

Saints also need to be awakened. It's very easy for us to slip into a spiritual sleep. No, it's not the sleep of our unconverted days; it's the sleep of indifference or apathy.

I'm sure that the Spirit of God alone can actually awaken

sleeping sinners and drowsy saints. But I'm equally sure that the Spirit of God is pleased to use human instruments to accomplish His purposes. He could work without us, but He has chosen to work through us. He can and does work through our words, our actions, our giving, and our prayers to do His awakening work.

Among the words the Spirit uses is the preaching of God's Word, the Bible. The Holy Spirit calls and equips preachers to be awakening agents.

What kind of preaching awakens people? It's not necessarily loud preaching, but an occasional break away from a chatty monotone would be welcome.

The need is rather for seriousness in preaching. Many preachers these days undercut any possibility of waking anybody up by presenting their messages in a very casual, lighthearted way. They seem to be saying: "I'm not very serious about this, and you shouldn't be, either." Listening to them never leaves the impression that they are preaching to eternity-bound people. Their primary concern appears to be getting their hearers to like them. They themselves are really the focus of their own sermons.

No preacher should set out to make his hearers dislike him. The need is rather for the preacher to step to one side so that the people can focus on God. The preacher who insists on showcasing his own cuteness and cleverness will find it hard to get the listeners to think about anything else.

I recall the story of a well-known man going to hear the great George Whitefield preach. When the service was over, someone asked him if Whitefield had convinced him to believe. The man replied: "No, but he convinced me that *he* believes."

The first task of the preacher may very well be to convince his hearers that he believes. He certainly can't expect to convince them to believe if he doesn't first convince them that he believes. Believes what? That God is the holy judge before whom we must all stand and give account! That we are all totally unprepared for that meeting because we have sinned against God time after time! That God has graciously provided through His Son, the Lord Jesus Christ, the way for our sins to be forgiven so that we can stand before Him without fear when He judges! That what the Lord Jesus Christ did for sinners applies to us when we repent of our sins and trust wholly in His redeeming work! That being freed from the condemnation of our sins through Christ is such a wonderful thing that we should gladly devote ourselves to loving the Lord and living for the glory of His name!

In short, preachers are to be great believers in great truths. They are to be men who feel the weight of eternity, but many preachers these days leave the distinct impression that they are either unfamiliar or ill at ease with the central Christian message. Eternity doesn't seem to weigh heavily upon them. They seem to be more in tune with the times than they are with the truth.

Ours is a time of deep sleep. Sinners sleep in one way and saints in another. This time cries for awakening. But what if those charged with awakening others are asleep? How, then, can they be used to awaken anyone else?

-3-

From God's Word, the Bible...

*Now the word of the LORD came to Jonah
the son of Amittai, saying. . .*

Jonah 1:1

"The word of the LORD came"

"The word of the LORD came to Jonah, the son of Amittai...." Now things are different for Jonah. His life is no longer the same. His nest of comfort has been torn up. Everything is now in disarray. Why? Because the word of the Lord that came to Jonah said something that he didn't want it to say. It told him to go to Nineveh, the capital city of Assyria, and "cry out against it" (v. 2). Nineveh, that "great city" was great in wickedness, and the Lord was fed up with both the city and its wickedness.

But that word from the Lord displeased Jonah. He didn't like it. You're thinking that Jonah had such a soft, easygoing spirit that he couldn't bear the thought of God threatening to judge people. But, no, that wasn't it. To the contrary, Jonah, the Jewish prophet, would have welcomed judgment for the Ninevites, who were the sworn enemies of his people. If they were told to repent, they might repent; and if they repented, the judgment Jonah wanted to come wouldn't come.

~ 25 ~

So Jonah was face to face with the unpleasant word of God.

We shouldn't think the story of Jonah has nothing to do with us. The word of God still comes to us today. I can't say for sure how the word of the Lord came to Jonah. Was it by God speaking out loud? Or was it by a deep, inner persuasion? I don't know. But I can tell you the principal way that the word of God comes today. It comes through Scripture. Yes, the Bible is God's book. He caused it to be written, and He speaks through it to us. He tells us what He wants us to do and what He wants us not to do.

What a marvel the Bible is! It consists of sixty-six books written by approximately forty men over a period of 1,600 years. And these forty men came from many walks of life and represented various levels of learning. David and Solomon were kings. Paul was a scholarly rabbi. Peter and John, on the other hand, were common, ordinary fishermen, and Matthew was a tax collector.

Those details wouldn't be so impressive if it weren't for the fact that all of these men over all those ages produced a book that has one glorious theme—God providing forgiveness for sinners through His Son, the Lord Jesus Christ.

Through the Bible, God speaks to us. He calls us to repent of our sins and trust in His Son. He calls us to see sin in all of its ugly reality and to hate it as He hates it. He calls us to see how helpless we are in dealing with our sin and to flee to the way of salvation that He has provided. He calls us to abandon our own wisdom and bow before His wisdom, the wisdom that He used to put together the plan of salvation.

God doesn't stop speaking to us in the Bible when we bow before Him in repentance and faith and receive His salvation. He tells us to live for His honor, praise, and glory after we're saved.

Some think they can avoid the word of the Lord. If they

don't read or hear it, they're not responsible for it! That's their reasoning. So they spend their lives as if God hasn't spoken at all or as if His words don't apply to them. All who think along such lines would do well to check with Jonah. The little book that bears his name exists to show us the utter folly of trying to avoid the word of the Lord. God speaks in the Bible whether we read it or hear it, and He holds us responsible for it even if we ignore it.

The book of Revelation tells us that on the great day of final judgment, certain "books" will be opened (Rev. 20:12). I don't doubt for a moment that the Bible will be among those books. On that day, people will be confronted with how God expected them to live and will be made to see how their lives measured up or failed to measure up.

Awesome thought! The Bible itself will be on hand to greet us when we go out into eternity. Let us heed it now so we don't have to fear it then.

-4-

From God's Word, the Bible...

And so we have the prophetic word confirmed, which you do well to heed as a light that shines in a dark place, until the day dawns and the morning star rises in your hearts; knowing this first, that no prophecy of Scripture is of any private interpretation, for prophecy never came by the will of man, but holy men of God spoke as they were moved by the Holy Spirit.

2 Peter 1:19-21

Why Believe the Bible?

The word of the Lord came to Jonah, and the word of the Lord still comes to people today. The primary way that we receive God's Word is through Scripture.

But how can we be sure that the Bible is really God's Word? I wasn't a Christian very long until I discovered that the Bible was widely rejected as the inspired Word of God. The impression that the skeptics created was that those who believed the Bible did so because they were ignorant know-nothings and not because there was any compelling evidence.

I soon learned that I had several substantial reasons for accepting the inspiration and authority of the Bible:

- its many, many fulfilled prophecies (Jesus Himself is estimated to have fulfilled 325 Old Testament prophecies. The mathematical probability of one man doing this is off the charts!);

- its survival even though it has been fiercely attacked;
- the changed lives of those who believe the Bible and seek to obey it;
- the correspondence of the Bible to what we observe all around us;
- the astounding discoveries of archaeologists.

These are very persuasive evidences. But the truly decisive thing for me was that Jesus obviously accepted the authority of the Scriptures, and Jesus was not just another man. The miracles that He performed and the way He spoke made it plain that He was the God-man, that is, God in human flesh. But the supreme proof of His identity was His own resurrection from the dead. Ordinary men don't come out of their graves, but Jesus came out of His grave, proving, as Paul says, that He was and is "the Son of God with power" (Rom. 1:4).

How can we be sure that Jesus actually arose from the dead? The tomb was empty. Many people saw Him, and many of them were changed by Him. Presented with such evidence, any unbiased jury could hand down only one verdict—Jesus arose!

With such evidence for such a person, doesn't it make sense to accept His testimony regarding the Bible? Even if it means I must set aside the conclusions of thousands of scholars, I will accept the testimony of Jesus. His credentials put Him in a class by Himself.

This is the Jesus who put His stamp of approval on Holy Scripture, and the question each believer must face is quite simple: how can we call Him our Lord if we reject what He taught about the Bible? We would also do well to ask this: if Jesus was wrong about the Bible, what else was He wrong about?

It's clear that Jesus endorsed the Old Testament during

His public ministry. He explicitly affirmed its authority (Matt. 5:17-18; John 10:35). In His controversies with the religious leaders, He appealed to it as His authority (e.g., Matt. 22:23-33). He also seems to have gone out of His way to certify those parts of it that are most often dismissed as myths. Adam and Eve (Matt. 19:4-5), Noah and the ark (Matt. 24:37-39), the fiery judgment on Sodom and the terrible fate of Lot's wife (Luke 17:28-32), the miraculous ministries of Elijah and Elisha (Luke 4:25-27), Jonah and the great fish (Matt. 12:39-41)—all were treated by Jesus as historical facts.

But what about the New Testament? It wasn't in existence during Jesus' ministry. Are we supposed to believe that He accepted something that didn't exist?

This brings us to the concept of pre-endorsement. This means that Jesus assured in advance that the New Testament would indeed be the infallible Word of God. He did so by promising His disciples that the Holy Spirit would call things to their remembrance, thus providing for the Gospel accounts (John 14:26); would guide them into all truth, thus providing for the epistles (John 16:13); and would show them things to come, thus providing for the book of Revelation (John 16:13).

So no matter where we turn in Scripture, we may rest assured that the Lord Jesus Himself has, as it were, initialed every page!

And the same Holy Spirit who caused the Bible to be written works within us to convince us that it is God's Word. We don't believe the Bible simply because the Bible tells us to believe the Bible but rather because the Spirit of God tells us to believe it as we read it.

-5-

From God's Word, the Bible...

All Scripture is given by inspiration of God, and is profitable for doctrine, for reproof, for correction, for instruction in righteousness, that the man of God may be complete, thoroughly equipped for every good work.

2 Timothy 3:16-17

How the Word of God Comes to Us (1)

"The word of the LORD came to Jonah, the son of Amittai...." And, as we've noticed, God's Word comes to us primarily through the Bible.

The Bible speaks to us in various ways. One is the way that a doctor speaks to his or her patients. That manner of speaking generally consists of two parts—diagnosis and prescription.

The Bible speaks to us in those same ways. First, there is *the diagnostic way*. As a doctor diagnoses the physical condition of his or her patient, so the Bible diagnoses our spiritual condition.

With our physical condition, the main thing we want from our doctor is the truth. We don't want him or her to sweep the truth under the rug because we might find that truth to be unpleasant. If a doctor did that, we would soon offer a two-word diagnosis of our own: bad doctor!

The Bible is a good doctor. It tells us the truth about

ourselves—very unpleasant truth! It tells us that we are all sinners (Rom. 3:23), and that our sins merit the judgment of God (Rom. 6:23). We were made by God to live for the glory and the honor of His name. We were to do that by worshiping and obeying Him. But sin pulls us away from that grand purpose. It causes us to worship ourselves and to rebel against God's commandments.

In the previous reading, I mentioned that one reason to believe the Bible is that it corresponds to what we see around us. When I take a long look at the world and at myself, I see the sinfulness that the Bible tells me about.

The Bible also comes to us in *a prescriptive way*. Doctors diagnose diseases, and they prescribe treatments for those diseases.

The Bible very emphatically declares that we are sinners, but it also prescribes a cure. That cure is the Lord Jesus Christ. He came to this earth for the specific purpose of healing or saving sinners (Matt. 1:21; Luke 19:10).

What exactly did Jesus do? He first took our humanity. As one of us, He could do something for us or on our behalf. In our humanity, He lived without sin. Since He had no sin of His own to pay for, He could pay for the sins of others. And pay He did! On the cross He received the penalty for sinners so all who believe in Him don't have to pay that same penalty themselves. But that's not all. After He died on the cross, He arose from the grave. In so doing, He proved that He was indeed God in human flesh, and that His death on the cross did indeed provide the salvation that sinners need.

What Jesus did in His living, dying, and rising is the way of salvation. Please notice that it is "the way," not "a way" (John 14:6; Acts 4:12; 1 Tim. 2:5-6). This teaching disturbs lots of people. In their opinion, to say that there is only one way of salvation is to be narrow-minded, bigoted, and intolerant.

But if these same people were to be told by their doctors

that they have a very serious disease for which there is only one cure, they would be glad for that cure! They wouldn't fuss and fume about it, and they wouldn't refuse to accept it because there weren't a dozen other cures.

For the horrible disease of sin, I don't need a dozen cures. I only need one. And if Jesus is the cure, I say: "Let me have Jesus." And I can have Him by repenting of my sins and trusting in what He did for sinners. You can have Him too!

So the Bible comes to us in a diagnostic way, telling us about our sins. And it comes to us in a prescriptive way, telling us about what the Lord Jesus did and urging us to believe in Him. It's not surprising, then, that John Burton could write these words:

> *Holy Bible, Book divine,*
> *Precious treasure, thou art mine;*
> *Mine to tell me whence I came;*
> *Mine to teach me what I am;*
> *Mine to chide me when I rove;*
> *Mine to show a Savior's love. . . .*

-6-

From God's Word, the Bible...

The LORD is my shepherd;
I shall not want.
He makes me to lie down in green pastures;
He leads me beside the still waters.
He restores my soul;
He leads me in the paths of righteousness
For His name's sake.
Yea, though I walk through the valley of the shadow of death,
I will fear no evil;
For You are with me;
Your rod and Your staff, they comfort me.

Psalm 23:1-4

How the Word of God Comes to Us (2)

We have noticed that the Word of God comes to us as a doctor to diagnose and prescribe. We can also say that it comes to us as a shepherd. The Lord Jesus, who is the Good Shepherd, uses the Word of God to shepherd us.

The Bible refers to God's people as sheep (Ps. 95:7; 100:3; John 10:26-30). We probably shouldn't take this as a compliment. Sheep are rather dumb and helpless. They are easy prey for predators, and they easily stray.

Sheep need a shepherd. They can't survive and thrive without one. The shepherd does four main things for his sheep. He feeds them, protects them, guides them, and finds them when they stray.

The Lord Jesus, who is the Good Shepherd, uses the Word of God to shepherd us. He *feeds* us with it. It is the food that God has developed and designed for our spiritual growth and health (1 Peter 2:2).

Psalm 23:1 refers to the shepherd making his sheep lie

down in green pastures. The Word of God is our green pasture. If we don't feed on it as we should, we make ourselves scrawny sheep.

The Lord also *protects* us through God's Word. Just as there are predators who are eager to dine on sheep, so God's people are constantly surrounded with spiritual predators who are happy to dine on them.

The Bible protects us from these spiritual predators by first telling us that they exist. The Bible often warns us about false teachers. It also informs us about the nature of their teachings (2 Cor. 11:1-4, 13-15; Gal. 1:6-9; Phil. 3:1-2, 17-19; 2 Peter 2:1-22; 1 John 4:1-3; Jude 3-19).

False teachers are very subtle. They don't blatantly announce that they are false teachers who are out to undermine and destroy our faith. They may very well profess to love the Bible. The key thing to keep in mind is what they do with the Bible. Do they accurately proclaim its message? The Bible's main subject is the redeeming work of Christ. When we are listening to preachers and teachers, we should always ask ourselves if they are exalting Christ in the same way that the Bible does. Are they proclaiming His supernatural birth, His sinless life, His substitutionary and sacrificial death, His stunning resurrection and ascension, and His soon-coming return?

The Lord also *guides* us with the Word of God. Psalm 23 refers to the Lord leading His sheep "beside still waters" (v. 2). Because sheep won't drink from turbulent water, the shepherd must use large stones to stop the current and create quiet waters so the sheep can drink and be refreshed. The Lord uses His Word to calm and refresh our spirits. Psalm 23 also mentions the shepherd leading his sheep in "the paths of righteousness" (v. 3). The Bible tells us what righteous living is, namely, conforming our lives to its teachings. It shows us the blessings that come our way when we engage in righteous living, and the heartaches that come our way when we don't.

The Bible guides us to righteous living by giving us both negative and positive commands, that is, it tells us not to do certain things, and it tells us to do certain things. It also gives us examples of people who lived righteously and of those who didn't.

Finally, the Lord also *finds* His straying sheep by using His Word. In Psalm 23:3, David mentions the Lord restoring his soul.

Sheep are always prone to stray, as Jonah did. But the Lord doesn't give up on us when we stray. We don't cease to be His sheep when we stray. Once a sheep, always a sheep! That's how it is with us when we belong to Him. When we stray, He doesn't re-save us, but He does restore us. And He often uses the Word of God to do so. He may cause one of its warnings to suddenly spring to mind. Or He may remind us of one of His promises. He may even prompt us to think of the experience of Jonah and to determine that we are going to follow Jesus and not Jonah.

As the word of the Lord came to Jonah, so it comes to God's people today in a shepherdly way. How very blessed we are to have it! May God help us to heed it!

-7-

From God's Word, the Bible...

Now the word of the LORD came to Jonah the son of Amittai, saying, "Arise, go to Nineveh, that great city, and cry out against it; for their wickedness has come up before Me." But Jonah arose to flee to Tarshish from the presence of the LORD. He went down to Joppa, and found a ship going to Tarshish; so he paid the fare, and went down into it, to go with them to Tarshish from the presence of the LORD.

Jonah 1:1-3

Races and Runners

The word of the Lord came, and Jonah went—in exactly the opposite direction! He found a ship going to Tarshish. Many commentators think this Tarshish was located in Spain.

Take a glance at a map, and you easily get the picture. Jonah was in Israel. Nineveh was east of there in Assyria, and Tarshish was west of Israel in Spain. And Spain was not just a little west of Israel. It was *really* west.

So Jonah's decision to go to Spain was disobedience with an exclamation point. Jonah wasn't merely refusing to go to Nineveh. He was going to get as far away from it as possible. Jonah's answer to serving God in the far East was to go to the far West!

There was a time when Jonah ran for God and ran well. God would say, "Go there," and he would go. God would say, "Go over yonder," and Jonah would go (2 Kings 14:25).

But God has now commanded him to go to Nineveh, and he is running away. Was he running from his responsibility? Yes, he certainly was. But verse 3 tells us two times that he was running "from the presence of the LORD."

This, then, is the connection we must make: when we run from obedience, we run from God.

Some seem to have the idea that they can live close to God and disobey His commands. It isn't so. To run from God's commands is to run from God Himself. Those who think that they can throw down their spiritual responsibilities at the drop of a hat and still be close to God are fooling themselves. We have a tendency to assume that we are close to God if we have warm, fuzzy feelings about Him. But the Lord doesn't leave us to define for ourselves what constitutes closeness to Him. He defines it for us, and His definition includes obedience to His commands (Luke 6:46).

The first part of Jonah's story, then, is the story of God setting a race before Jonah, and Jonah refusing to run that race.

Jonah always makes me think of another runner in another race. Before this world saw its first day, God the Father said to His Son: "I have a race for You to run. It is the race of saving sinners. This race will require You to take their humanity and to live without sin in that humanity. It will cause You to be hated and despised by many, and to die on a Roman cross a special kind of death, one in which You will actually endure My wrath against sinners."

The Lord Jesus looked at the race set before Him by the Father and said: "I will run it." And run it He did! Without faltering or stumbling, He ran redemption's race until He burst across the finish line on the cross as He cried out: "It is finished!" (John 19:30). Had Jesus stopped short in His race, there would have been no salvation for any of us. But He didn't stop short. Thank God for Jesus, the faithful runner! He is the greatest runner who has run the greatest race.

All of us who have taken Jesus as our Lord and Savior now have our own race to run. It is the race of loving Him, worshipping Him, serving Him, trusting Him, and, yes, obeying Him. Our choice is ever to run the Jonah race or the Jesus race. The author of Hebrews urges us to run the latter: ". . . let us lay aside every weight, and the sin which so easily ensnares us, and let us run with endurance the race that is set before us, looking unto Jesus, the author and finisher of our faith, who for the joy that was set before Him, endured the cross, despising the shame, and has sat down at the right hand of the throne of God" (Heb. 12:1b-2).

Jonah refused to run the Jesus race. He ran the Jonah race, and he ran into trouble. We can be assured that he would now tell each of us to not do as he did. He would tell us to run the Jesus race, no matter what the cost.

-8-

From God's Word, the Bible...

You ran well. Who hindered you from obeying the truth?

Galatians 5:7

Why Jonah Ran

Why did Jonah run from God? On *the surface level*, we must say Jonah didn't love those whom God loved. God loved the Ninevites (Jonah 4:2). Jonah didn't. Jonah wanted the Ninevites to be None-evites. As far as he was concerned, it was a good thing for God to be planning to bring judgment upon them. If there were no Ninevites, they could never be a threat to the people of Israel.

It's never a good thing when we try to do God's thinking for Him, and that's exactly what we like to do. When it comes to the governing of the affairs of this world, we want to come alongside God and say: "Let me help You with that."

We need to realize that God does His own thinking, and His thinking is never mistaken. Elihu was certainly right to ask of God:

> *Who has assigned Him His way,*
> *Or who has said, "You have done wrong"?*
> (Job 36:23)

Centuries later, the prophet Isaiah similarly asked:

> *Who has directed the Spirit of the LORD,*
> *Or as His counselor has taught Him?*
> (Isa. 40:13)

The Apostle Paul may have been thinking of the questions of both Elihu and Isaiah when he wrote:

> *For who has known the mind of the Lord:*
> *Or who has become His counselor?*
> (Rom. 11:34)

God told Jonah to go to Nineveh, and Jonah essentially said to God: "You can't mean that!" In regard to the things of God, those words can easily pop into our minds and burst from our lips. They may very well do so more frequently in connection with the cross of Christ than with any other matter. When God points to His Son dying on the cross and declares that as our only hope for salvation, many want to say to Him: "You can't mean that!"

That cross makes no sense at all to us if the Spirit of God doesn't enlighten us (1 Cor. 2:14). A man dying on a cross is the way for us to have our sins forgiven and to go to heaven? How ridiculous! And we are supposed to come humbly to that cross repenting of our sins, trusting in what Jesus did there, and renouncing every other hope for salvation? Absurd! We are intelligent, sophisticated human beings, and we refuse to accept such ludicrous teaching!

After all of our posturing and pontificating and our ranting and raging, God still points to that cross and says: "That's My way of salvation!" To everyone who says to Him: "You can't mean that," God simply says: "I most certainly do!" And those of us who have been rescued from our sins by that cross gladly chime in with the Apostle Paul: "For the message of the cross is foolishness to those who are perishing, but to us who are being saved it is the power of God" (1 Cor. 1:18).

Psalm 2 powerfully pictures this for us. The great people of the earth "take counsel together" against God and His Son and arrogantly assert that they are not going to bow in submission. How does the Lord respond? Does He fly into a panic? Hardly. He rather laughs at them and says:

> *Yet I have set My King*
> *On the holy hill of Zion.*
> (Ps. 2:6)

We don't have to be among the great people of this earth to make their great mistake. Whether great or small, the person who thinks he or she knows better than God had better think again.

We must also go to *a deeper level* to explain Jonah's running. I will put it bluntly: he was a backslider.

Backsliding used to be a commonly used word. It's not so common any more. But the fact that the word has become rare doesn't mean that backsliding itself has become rare.

What is backsliding? It is the Christian losing ground. It's not him or her losing salvation. That can never be! (John 10:27-30; Phil. 1:6). It's rather the Christian sliding back or slipping back from where he or she once was and ought still to be. It's the Christian slipping in love, that is, loving the highest thing (God) less and loving lower things more.

By including the account of Jonah in the Bible, God put backsliding in all of its ugliness on display so we can see it, be repulsed by it, and not do it.

-9-

From God's Word, the Bible...

Yet they did not obey or incline their ear, but followed the counsels and the dictates of their evil hearts, and went backward and not forward.

And they have turned to Me the back, and not the face; though I taught them, rising up early and teaching them, yet they have not listened to receive instruction.

Jeremiah 7:24; Jeremiah 32:33

Backsliding

Since Jonah has brought up the subject of backsliding, we need to consider it. Why consider something so unpleasant and distasteful? One reason is its prominence in Scripture. Verses that use some form of the word "backslide" appear seventeen times in the Bible. Then there are the other words that the Bible uses for backsliding such as "forsake" (appearing approximately fifty times) and "depart" (Isa. 59:13; Heb. 3:12). Then we have the sad accounts of saints who backslid at some point. Noah, Lot, Jacob, Samson, David, Solomon, and Simon Peter all come readily to mind.

Another reason is that the subject is of practical importance. The wellbeing of our families, our churches, our nation, and ourselves all hinge to a large degree on God's people staying close to Him.

In the previous reading, we defined backsliding as the Christian slipping back or sliding back from where he or she once was and ought still to be.

Let's take a stroll down memory lane to that time

when we were converted. Conversion means change, and there is no more radical change than becoming a Christian. The Apostle Paul likens it to becoming a new creature (2 Cor. 5:17).

Conversion radically changed our thinking. We came to see ourselves as guilty sinners before a holy God. We saw ourselves facing eternal destruction, and we came to understand that Christ's atoning death on the cross was the only way that we could be freed from God's wrath. How exceedingly precious the gospel was to us in those days!

Conversion also profoundly changed our desires. Sinful things lost their luster as we began to enjoy God's Word, prayer, and church services. We had a zeal for God and a desire and determination to do His work. We also had a love for God's people and a desire for others to know Him.

Conversion also changed our behavior. We began to order our lives in keeping with God's commandments. Old habits melted away as we began giving priority to pleasing God.

Backsliding affects each of those areas. Our thinking is not as much in tune with God's Word as it was. The gospel doesn't seem quite as precious to us as it once did. Our desires are also affected. We discover that we don't have our hearts in serving the Lord. Coldness has set in. Zeal has been replaced with a lack of interest. Our behavior is also affected as we go back to some of the sinful behavior that we had laid aside.

Conversion to Christ consists of a forsaking, on the one hand, and an embracing on the other. In conversion we radically broke with our sins, our false gods, and our worldly thinking and doing to embrace God as the only true God and our rightful sovereign. We took His ways as our ways, His laws as our laws, His cause as our cause, His people as our people and His Word as our authority.

Backsliding is going back to embrace those things we forsook for God. It is a forsaking of God for those things that we once forsook for Him.

What causes us to backslide? We know that we have a very powerful and clever enemy, the devil. If he can't prevent us from coming to Christ, the next best thing for him is to prevent us from living as a Christian ought to live. The Apostle Peter portrays him as a prowling lion who is seeking to devour Christians (1 Peter 5:8).

We also know that the world is very strong and alluring. It is always exerting pressure on us to conform to its thinking and doing (Rom. 12:2). It's a sad fact that many individual Christians, many pastors, and many churches seem to fear being out of step with the world. The latest opinion poll seems to be more important to them than the Bible.

We also know that our flesh is very weak, causing us to crave those things that "war against the soul" (1 Peter 2:11).

The Lord Jesus was "in all points tempted as we are," yet He did not sin (Heb. 4:15). Jesus knew all about the devil, the world, and the flesh. He was confronted by the strength of each, but He didn't waver. He forged ahead to complete the work of redemption. The more we look to Him, the less inclined we will be to backslide.

-10-

From God's Word, the Bible...

Watch, stand fast in the faith, be brave, be strong.

Be sober, be vigilant; because your adversary the devil walks about like a roaring lion, seeking whom he may devour. Resist him, steadfast in the faith, knowing that the same sufferings are experienced by your brotherhood in the world.

1 Corinthians 16:13; 1 Peter 5:8-9

Watch!

Jonah's experience of backsliding warns all us who know the Lord to be watch ourselves. All of us are watching certain things. I don't mean to say that we never take our eyes off these things, but rather we are continually aware of them and prepared to take appropriate action to preserve and protect them. We watch our appearance, our manners, our children, our reputations, our possessions, our health, our driving, and so on. People used to watch their language, but that particular watching seems to be less and less common.

Think about all of these watchings. What do they have in common? When we say we're watching something, what are we really saying? Aren't we affirming in each case that something we value could very well be threatened in such a way that we would be deprived of our enjoyment of it? We value our health, but we're always aware that there are threats to it that we must guard against, so we can continue to enjoy it. The Bible teaches us that a close walk with God is something of real value that is constantly being threatened. It is something that we can be deprived of if we aren't awake and alert.

How valuable is it to walk close to God? If we fail to do so, we:

- cause Him to be displeased with us (Eph. 4:30; 1 Thess. 5:19);
- bring a hardness into our own hearts (Ps. 95:7-8);
- bring harm to others (2 Sam. 12:14);
- rob ourselves of spiritual comfort and assurance (Ps. 32:3-4);
- invite God to visit us with chastisement (Heb. 12:7; 1 Cor. 11:31-32).

It's plain, isn't it? A close walk with God is worth watching. So let's watch. Let's watch our prayer life. How easy it is to be careless here! It's easy to say: "I know that I should pray, but I just don't feel like doing it." The key is to pray until we do feel like doing it. When Simon Peter, James, and John didn't feel like praying in the Garden of Gethsemane, Jesus said to them: "Watch and pray, lest you enter into temptation. The spirit truly is ready, but the flesh is weak" (Mark 14:38).

Let's watch our church attendance. If we've been cutting back, we must devote ourselves afresh to being faithful. I'm always astonished when I hear someone say that there aren't any commands in the Bible for us to attend church. Every time I hear that I call to mind these words: "And let us consider one another in order to stir up love and good works, not forsaking the assembling of ourselves together, as is the manner of some. . . ." (Heb. 10:24-25a).

Let's watch how we respond while we in the services of the church. Do we allow ourselves to be distracted by other things and preoccupied with other things? We all know that it is very easy to be present in church without really being present. Over the years, I have frequently noticed among those who attend services what I call "the donut effect." While they are present, they are "glazed over." They don't know or appreciate what is going on in the service because they are not really there.

All too often we let duty swallow up delight. We attend services because we regard this as our duty to do so, but we take no delight in the services. We listen to the preaching because it is our duty to do so, but we don't delight in the truth of God.

Let's make sure we dwell much on the cost of walking afar off from God. It is, as noted above, a costly thing.

Let's make sure that we dwell much on what the Lord Jesus Christ did for us when He died on the cross. And when it comes time to observe the Lord's Supper, let's be sure that we are present—really present—to think deeply with profound gratitude about the Lord Jesus going to the cross to shed His blood for us. The cross of Christ, rightly perceived, always warms our hearts and wards off coldness. It is always our greatest protection against backsliding.

Jesus, keep me near the cross,
There a precious fountain
Free to all—a healing stream,
Flows from Calvary's mountain.

In the cross, in the cross,
Be my glory ever;
Till my raptured soul shall find
Rest beyond the river.
(Fanny J. Crosby)

If we want to watch against backsliding, we must watch the cross.

-11-

From God's Word, the Bible...

But the LORD sent out a great wind on the sea, and there was a mighty tempest on the sea, so that the ship was about to be broken up.

Jonah 1:4

Storms and Sleepers

If we take one step down the wrong road, it may be very hard for us to find an exit ramp. Jonah took one step on the wrong road when he thought that he knew better than God on the matter of the Ninevites. He took another step on that same road when he actually thought he could escape from God.

For a while, Jonah must have thought that he had succeeded. Everything seemed to fall into place. He apparently journeyed from Gath-Hepher to Joppa without incident. He found a ship that was sailing far from Israel. He had enough money to pay the fare. The ship soon got underway. Jonah was able to go to sleep in the hold of the ship. And there was no sign of God anywhere! Perhaps God had changed His plan to send a prophet to Nineveh. Or perhaps He had found Himself another prophet. Whatever the case, Jonah was off the hook—or so it seemed!

Many years ago, a popular song featured this line: "I fought the law, and the law won." Jonah was about to learn in very dramatic and powerful ways that the one who fights God ends up singing: "I fought the Lord, and the Lord won."

Jonah's experience on the ship gives us insight into the nature of God. For one thing, God is all-knowing. He never needs information. He didn't need anyone to tell Him about Jonah's slipping and sleeping, that is, his slipping down to Joppa and sleeping in the ship.

And God is all-powerful. When He wants to do something, He never lacks the resources to get it done. In Jonah's case, God had a storm, the ship's captain and crew, and a fish all lined up and waiting.

If we could only keep in our minds the all-seeing, powerful God, it would surely keep us from many foolish thoughts, words, and deeds, and from the many heartaches produced by those things.

First came the storm. A frightful one it was! The wind was so "great" and the tempest so "mighty" that "the ship was about to be broken up."

That storm came directly from God! It was "sent out" by Him. The words "sent out" translate a Hebrew word that means "hurled." Get this picture: Jonah is blissfully sleeping in a ship, and God takes dead aim at that ship and hurls this storm toward it as a man would hurl a javelin.

Wasn't God being rather vindictive and vengeful toward Jonah? Will you be surprised if I say God hurled that storm toward His disobedient prophet with a heart of love? It was love that refused to let Jonah go. It was love that was determined to bring him back. How thankful we should be for divine love that refuses to give up on us!

> *O Love that wilt not let me go,*
> *I rest my weary soul in Thee;*
> *I give Thee back the life I owe,*
> *That in Thine ocean depths its flow*
> *May richer, fuller be.*
> (George Matheson)

The storm raging and Jonah sleeping! That calls to mind another boat, another storm, and another sleeper. Jesus was in a boat with His disciples when "a great tempest arose on the sea" (Matt. 8:24). While the storm raged, Jesus slept. But with those details we come to the end of the similarities with the prophet. Jonah was sleeping to escape a demanding ministry. The Lord Jesus slept as a result of meeting the many demands of ministry (Matt 8:1-22). And the storm in which Jonah slept came to correct him. The storm in which Jesus slept came as an opportunity for Him to correct His disciples for their little faith and for them to see more of His glory (Matt. 8:26-27). Also, the storm in which Jonah found himself stopped when he was thrown overboard (Jonah 1:15). The storm that came upon Jesus stopped as a result of His command and while He was still in the boat.

What a difference between Jonah and Jesus! Having had crucial work set before him, Jonah played the part of an escapee. But Jesus never tried to escape from the work the Father set before Him. Instead of turning from it, He set His face toward it. Because He didn't try to escape God's commands, all who turn to Him in repentance and faith can escape their sins and condemnation.

-12-

From God's Word, the Bible...

So the captain came to him, and said to him, "What do you mean, sleeper? Arise, call on your God; perhaps your God will consider us, so that we may not perish."
And they said to one another, "Come, let us cast lots, that we may know for whose cause this trouble has come upon us." So they cast lots, and the lot fell on Jonah. Then they said to him, "Please tell us! For whose cause is this trouble upon us? What is your occupation? And where do you come from? What is your country? And of what people are you?"
So he said to them, "I am a Hebrew; and I fear the LORD, the God of heaven, who made the sea and the dry land."

Jonah 1:6-9
(Read the whole passage in Jonah 1:4-16.)

The Captain and the Crew

It's one thing to run. It's quite another to escape. Jonah had run from God, but he hadn't escaped Him. God was in pursuit, and God always pursues faster than we can flee.

As noted in the previous reading, God had His instruments all lined up for bringing Jonah back to where he needed to be. First in line was the storm. Then came the captain of the ship, his crew, and the casting of lots.

God used the captain to rebuke Jonah for sleeping when he should have been praying. Ouch! A pagan rebuking a child of God for not praying!

I wonder when Jonah last prayed—really prayed! Backsliding and praying don't go hand in hand. If we pray, we don't backslide. If we backslide, we don't pray. Jonah had been backsliding

God also used the crew to wring from Jonah the truth about himself. Sad, isn't it, when a child of God conceals his faith from unbelievers!

The crewmembers somehow sensed that there was something unusual about this storm. They weren't willing to chalk it up to mere chance. They were convinced that this storm was someone's fault, and they were determined to discover the guilty party by casting lots.

Jonah knew he didn't have a chance when those lots were cast. He knew why the storm had come. It was the Lord who had sent it because of his disobedience, and he also knew whose hand would direct the hand that cast those lots. It was God's hand, and, just as Jonah expected, the lot fell on him, and the sailors demanded an explanation from Jonah. Then the truth came out. Jonah identified himself as a Hebrew and as a servant of the Lord and told them that he had "fled from the presence of the LORD" (v. 10).

So the sailors now knew the reason for the storm. It was Jonah. But what were they to do with him? Jonah solved the problem for them. The only way for them to calm the tempest was to throw him overboard (v. 12). Those sailors tried to spare him, but the storm only increased in its ferocity. The only thing left to do was what Jonah asked them to do.

So the prophet who was unwilling to save the pagans of Nineveh now saves the lives of these pagan sailors by laying down his life. As we know, it didn't actually cost Jonah his life, but he surely thought it would. This must surely make us think of the One greater than Jonah who was never for one moment unwilling to save the godless. This One knew for sure that He would have to lay down His life to save sinners, and lay it down He did. His name is Jesus (John 15:13).

Jonah correctly thought that he would save the lives of those sailors by laying down his life. What he didn't know until later was that he was also saving their souls. He was no sooner overboard than the storm ceased, and those men turned to the God of Jonah in true faith (v. 16).

We read no more of these men in Scripture, but it could very well be that they went on to Spain and there planted the seeds of the gospel.

What a joy it will be to meet these men in heaven and hear each one give his own account of a dreadful storm, a disobedient prophet, and God's saving grace!

This part of Jonah's story is dripping with irony. Jonah, who should have been a man of prayer, has to be told by a pagan captain to pray. Jonah, a man of God who should have always been eager to confess his identity and his God, has to have that confession wrung from him. And Jonah, unwilling to be part of saving the pagans in Nineveh, is used by God to save pagans on a ship.

Have we learned from Jonah? Have we learned to constantly guard against backsliding? Have we learned to ever nurture the life of prayer? Have we learned to always be ready to confess our faith? Have we learned to desire the salvation of all sinners? Most importantly, have we learned to look beyond Jonah, the unwilling prophet, to the One who is greater than Jonah, that is, the Lord Jesus Christ, who earnestly desires the salvation of sinners?

-13-

From God's Word, the Bible...

Now the LORD had prepared a great fish to swallow Jonah. And Jonah was in the belly of the fish three days and three nights.

Jonah 1:17

One Big Gulp

If Jonah thought he would perish in the sea, he was in for a huge surprise. That huge surprise came in the form of a huge fish. That fish was the last in the string of instruments that God had lined up to bring His backsliding prophet to obedience.

When Jonah hit the water, the fish was waiting. That fish gulped Jonah down without so much as a spoonful of tartar sauce! One big gulp was all that it took. One big gulp and Jonah was down. Farther down than he had ever been before. Farther down than he ever thought he could go. Down into the belly of a fish, and into the depths of the sea!

Are we really supposed to believe this happened? I respond to that by asking this question: Do we own Jesus as our Lord? If we do, we must not deny that Jonah was swallowed by that great fish because Jesus Himself used this account to affirm His own resurrection (Matt. 12:39-40). To deny the fish, we must deny the teaching of the Lord.

Let's say for a moment that Jonah was NOT actually swallowed by the fish. We can agree that Jesus either didn't know this or that He did. Now *if Jesus didn't know* that Jonah wasn't swallowed, Jesus was mistaken because He obviously thought something occurred that didn't.

But what *if Jesus knew* that Jonah wasn't swallowed by the fish? That would make Jesus devious in that He used something He knew didn't happen to convince His followers that His resurrection would happen.

So if we say Jonah wasn't actually swallowed by the fish, we must choose between a mistaken Jesus (who thought Jonah was swallowed) or a devious Jesus (who knew Jonah wasn't swallowed but acted as if he were).

The Lord Jesus was not mistaken or devious. He knew the truth about Jonah, and the truth was that Jonah was swallowed by the great fish and was, therefore, a most appropriate and fitting picture of Jesus' soon-coming resurrection.

Did Jonah actually die while he was in the fish? It could be that he did. If so, God resurrected him, and that would certainly make him an even more perfect picture of the resurrection of Jesus. We can ask Jonah in heaven.

One thing we know for sure is that Jonah prayed while he was in the fish. We may be surprised that Jonah was swallowed by a fish. We surely aren't surprised that Jonah prayed from that fish. How he prayed! It would help us to pray if we would keep in mind that God always has ways to bring us to prayer. Let's discipline ourselves to pray so the Lord won't have to discipline us to pray.

There is tremendous encouragement from Jonah praying while he was in the belly of the fish. He shows us that we can pray from any place or from any set of circumstances, and still be heard by God. When we feel as if we are in the belly of a whale all on our own, we can pray. What a consolation!

The way to read the book of Jonah is to keep one eye on Jonah and the other eye on Jesus. As we read about the prophet plummeting into the depths of the sea because of his disobedience to God, our minds should be drawn to Jesus on the cross. It was there that Jesus plummeted into the immeasurable depths of God's wrath. But Jesus plummeted into those depths, not because of His disobedience to God, but rather because of ours (Rom. 5:6,8; 2 Cor. 5:21; 1 Pet. 2:24). Jonah went unwillingly into the abyss for God to accomplish a great purpose. The Lord Jesus went down to far greater depths for God to accomplish a far greater purpose.

There is, as we noted above, another link between Jonah and Jesus. The fish wasn't the final resting place for Jonah, and the grave wasn't the final resting place for Jesus. He burst from His grave in glorious resurrection life, and He lives today.

Up from the grave He arose,
With a mighty triumph over His foes;
He arose a victor from the dark domain,
And He lives forever with His saint to reign.
He arose! He arose!
Hallelujah! Christ arose!
(Robert Lowry)

-14-

From God's Word, the Bible...

Then Jonah prayed to the LORD his God from the fish's belly. And he said:
"I cried out to the LORD because of my affliction,
And He answered me.
"Out of the belly of Sheol I cried,
And You heard my voice.
For You cast me into the deep,
Into the heart of the seas,
And the floods surrounded me;
All Your billows and Your waves passed over me."

Jonah 2:1-3
(Read the whole passage in Jonah 2:1-9.)

# Jonah's Revival

Some have described the events recorded in Jonah 3 as the greatest revival in history. What occurred in Nineveh, wonderful as it was, cannot accurately be called revival. It can certainly be called a spiritual awakening or even the result of revival, but not revival. The word "revival" means being restored to life, vitality, zeal or vigor. Revival is something that can only be experienced by God's people, and the Ninevites were pagans. Revival presupposes God's people being in a state of spiritual coldness and then being reinvigorated.

So the real revival in the book of Jonah is that which the prophet himself experienced while he was in the fish's belly. Before the fish swallowed him, Jonah was in a state of spiritual coldness and disobedience. While he was in that fish, he was spiritually renewed or restored.

Jonah 2 relates the prayer that Jonah prayed from the fish. Prayer is, of course, the primary means that God uses to revive His people (2 Chron. 7:14).

Let's notice three things about Jonah's prayer. First,

there is *the time of it*. We shouldn't rush past these words: "Then Jonah prayed to the LORD his God from the fish's belly" (v. 1).

These words tell us that God's chastisement of His prophet had achieved its purpose. The chastisement was severe. Jonah says he was in the belly of hell (v. 2), tucked away out of God's sight (v. 4), at the very bottom of the mountains (v. 6), where he felt locked up by the bars of the earth (v. 6).

Jonah describes the breadth of his chastisement by saying he was in the midst of waters on every side (v. 5). No matter where he looked, no end was in sight. He described the outward dimension of it by saying that weeds were wrapped around his head (v. 5), and he described the inward dimension of it by saying his soul fainted within (v. 7). His affliction touched both his body and his spirit.

We should also notice *the tone of the prayer*. Jonah twice says that he "cried." This is a word of energy, urgency, and fervency. It doesn't allow for half-heartedness. This is prayer with sweat on it.

One very large challenge these days is getting God's people to pray. Another large challenge is getting them to pray as they pray, that is, getting them to pray with fervency. We can be sure that revival hasn't yet come if we are content to mumble lazily in our prayers. When revival comes, the tone of prayer always changes.

The final thing for us to notice about Jonah's prayer is *the type that it was*.

It was very much a prayer of confession. First, Jonah confessed his idolatry. He says: "They that observe lying vanities forsake their own mercy" (v. 8). The phrase "lying vanities" is the Bible's frequent way of depicting idols as vain, empty delusions (Deut. 32:21; Jer. 10:14-15; 14:22).

But we don't read anywhere that Jonah had fallen down before a god of wood or stone to worship. So why did he confess idolatry? We must keep in mind that idolatry is putting anything in the place of God and giving it the honor and allegiance that belong to God. When Jonah disobeyed God, he was essentially placing his desires above God's commands. That's idolatry. Jonah's idol was himself.

Jonah also confessed the truth of God's sovereignty by saying: "Salvation is of the LORD" (v. 9).

Jonah has finally come to recognize what he should have understood at the outset and would have understood, had he not been so busy playing God himself. He sees that God, as the sovereign ruler of this universe, has the right to extend His mercy to whomever He wishes. Jonah had thought that the Ninevites were unworthy of salvation. He now sees from his own desperate situation that he is wholly dependent on God's mercy for deliverance while being, like the Ninevites, unworthy of that deliverance. If God were to deliver him, unworthy as *he* was, how could he dispute God's right to grant an even greater deliverance to the unworthy Ninevites?

Jonah was spiritually revived as he prayed. We should be thankful for his revival. We should be even more thankful for Jesus, who never needed revival because He never faltered in the work of redemption that the Father had given Him to do.

-15-

From God's Word, the Bible...

O Israel, return to the LORD your God,
For you have stumbled because of your iniquity;
Take words with you, And return to the LORD.
Say to Him, "Take away all iniquity;
Receive us graciously,
For we will offer the sacrifices of our lips.
Assyria shall not save us, We will not ride on horses,
Nor will we say anymore to the work of our hands,
'You are our gods.'
For in You the fatherless finds mercy."
"I will heal their backsliding,
I will love them freely,
For My anger has turned away from him."

Hosea 14:1-4

Experiencing Revival

The account of Jonah's revival in the belly of the fish summons us to consider the subject of revival more fully. Today we answer that summons by looking to another of the Old Testament prophets—Hosea. Hosea ministered to the nation of Israel from 754 to 714 B.C.

Throughout his prophecy, Hosea sounds the somber notes of sin and judgment. In this passage, he sounds the joyful note of hope. His message of hope is built around the word "return" (v. 1), a word he uses fifteen times in this prophecy. What a comforting word! We can come back to God! No matter how far we have strayed and how miserably we have failed, we can come back to God!

The people of Israel had turned their backs on God and had turned their faces toward sin. They had spurned God and embraced sin. The Lord here calls them to reverse what they had previously done. He calls them to turn their backs on their sins and turn their faces toward Him.

What He said to those backslidden Israelites speaks with equal force to us when we backslide.

First, He shows us *why we need to return to Him* (v. 1).

The people of Israel needed to return to God because they had "stumbled" because of their "iniquity."

Sin always makes us stumble. We cannot walk uprightly before God and walk in sin. We cannot walk close to God and walk in sin.

The New International Version translates the phrase "stumbled because of your iniquity" in this way: "Your sins have been your downfall!"

The devil would have us believe that sin is the way to happiness, satisfaction, and fulfillment. The truth is just the opposite. Sin is the way to heartache, misery, and ruin. Cain, Lot, Esau, Saul, and Judas Iscariot are some examples of men who painfully learned the truth about sin.

Hosea was not content to urge the people to return to God. He also declares *how we can return to Him* (vv. 2-3).

He says we are to "take words" with us. We must honestly talk to God about our sins.

This is what the prodigal son did when he returned to his father (Luke 15:21). This is what David did when he returned to the Lord after sinning so grievously (Ps. 51).

The Apostle John writes: "If we confess our sins, He is faithful and just to forgive us our sins and to cleanse us from all unrighteousness" (1 John 1 9).

It isn't enough, of course, to merely mouth empty words without sincerity of heart. Our words of repentance must come from hearts that are broken with the enormity of the sin. They must be words that ask God to take away the iniquity and to graciously forgive. They must include words of renunciation. As the nation of Israel was to renounce an alliance with Assyria as the means for achieving future security (v. 3), so our own return to God must feature a true renunciation of our dependence on every other resource as well as our idols.

Finally, the Lord tells us *what to expect when we return to Him* (v. 4).

The Lord assures us that He will "heal" our backsliding. What a wonderful thing healing is! Imagine someone who has suffered long from a painful, debilitating disease. He has had surgery and taken various treatments. Then one day his doctor says: "You can consider yourself to be healed."

That's essentially what God said to those people. Their backsliding was like a terrible disease. But God offered complete healing for it. He still heals backsliding today.

The Lord also assures us that He will love us "freely" when we return to Him (v. 4). We all know what it is to have people be cool and reserved toward us. God was promising to love His people warmly and without reserve. God receives backsliders spontaneously and warmly. He never makes returning difficult! Once again, we can look at the parable of the prodigal son for a picture of how God receives backsliders.

Let's remember that the God who loved us enough to put His Son on the cross for us doesn't stop loving us when we backslide. And when we backslide, let's seek true revival. Jonah's experience pictures it for us, and Hosea proclaims it to us. If we need revival, let's look to Jonah and listen to Hosea.

-16-

From God's Word, the Bible...

He is not here; for He is risen, as He said.
Come, see the place where the Lord lay.

Matthew 28:6

The Resurrection of Jesus

After Jonah experienced true spiritual renewal in the belly of the fish, he was "vomited . . . onto dry land" (Jonah 2:10).

We have been noting at various points that there is a link between Jonah's experience in the fish and the resurrection of Jesus. The former portrays the latter. This is not mere fanciful conjecture. The Lord Jesus Himself made the link in response to the Pharisees' request that He give them a sign. The only sign He gave them was "the sign of the prophet Jonah" (Matt. 12:38-39). Jesus then proceeded to say: "For as Jonah was three days and three nights in the belly of the great fish, so will the Son of Man be three days and three nights in the heart of the earth" (Matt. 12:40).

Someone may want to point out that Jesus didn't actually mention His resurrection in those words. True. But it is unquestionably implied. The Pharisees knew that Jonah didn't stay in the belly of the fish. So they had to know that Jesus was affirming that He would not stay in "the heart of the earth." By appealing to Jonah, Jesus was proclaiming His upcoming resurrection.

Let's first consider *what proves Jesus' resurrection*.

We need not be in doubt whether Jesus arose. The evidences for it are too many and too substantial. The stone of His tomb was rolled away. The tomb was empty. Those appointed to guard the tomb were in a stupor. Angels were present. The grave clothes of Jesus were left behind in a particularly convincing configuration. Many saw the risen Lord (500 on one occasion—see 1 Cor. 15:6)! And the disciples were changed from cowering wimps into bold evangelists.

If these evidences aren't enough for us, the problem is with us. If convincing evidence doesn't convince us, we just don't want to be convinced.

Why do some not want to be convinced? The answer is in our second consideration—*what Jesus' resurrection proves*.

The first thing is this: if Jesus arose from the dead, there can be no doubt that He was the person He claimed to be, namely, the God-man. Yes, Jesus emphatically claimed to be God in human flesh (John 14:9), and the resurrection proves it (Rom. 1:4). Ordinary men don't spring from their graves!

Why do people reject Jesus' resurrection? It means Jesus is God. That means He has authority over us. He can tell us how we ought to live and how we ought not to live. And we all want to live as we see fit. One man, when confronted with the powerful evidences for the Christian faith, was asked if he was willing to accept those evidences and receive Christ. His response was most telling: "No, I won't become a Christian, because I don't want the world to be like that."

Christianity says the world should bow before the authority of Jesus. That would make it quite different than what it is. And this man liked the sinful world the way it is. It wasn't the lack of evidence that drove him from

Christianity. It was the implications of the evidence.

The fact that we deny Jesus' resurrection doesn't destroy it. We can deny it and Jesus' lordship, but a day is coming in which the folly of such denial will be plain for all to see. On that day every knee will bow before Jesus, and every tongue will confess that He is Lord (Phil. 2:9-11).

A second thing that the resurrection proves is this: God was entirely satisfied with the death of Christ in the place of sinners. God is the One whom we have offended through our sins, and it is God who must be satisfied. The fact that God is the One who raised Jesus from the dead proves that God was satisfied with His redeeming death.

In one sense, the cross was the verdict of sinful men on Jesus. By nailing Him there, they were pronouncing Him to be a fraud. The resurrection was the verdict of God on Jesus, and what a radically different verdict it was! God was reversing or setting aside the verdict of sinful men on His Son, and pronouncing His own verdict on Him. By raising Jesus from the dead, God was setting the record straight regarding His Son.

Jonah points us to Jesus' resurrection, and Jesus' resurrection points us to what we should do with Jesus. We should bow humbly before Him as God and receive the gift of salvation that He achieved for us on the cross.

-17-

From God's Word, the Bible...

Then God saw their works, that they turned from their evil way; and God relented from the disaster that He had said He would bring upon them, and He did not do it.

Jonah 3:10
(Read the whole passage in Jonah 3:1-10.)

Re-sending, Repenting, and Relenting

The third chapter of Jonah seems to fall quite naturally into three parts: re-sending, repenting, and relenting. Jonah was re-sent, the Ninevites repented and God relented.

The fact that God re-issued his original call to Jonah is most encouraging. Our God is the God of the second chance, and the third and the fourth and. . . . God doesn't hold our sins and failures against us. When we repent, He forgives and forgets. The Apostle John wonderfully consoles us with these words about the Lord: "If we confess our sins, He is faithful and just to forgive us our sins and to cleanse us from all unrighteousness" (1 John 1:9).

There were once two men who became reconciled after being at odds with each other. When asked if it was true that they had buried the hatchet, one of these two men replied: "Yes, but I left the handle sticking up in case I need the hatchet again."

God never leaves the handle sticking up. How very

thankful we should be! The Lord could have left Jonah to perish in the sea or in the fish, but He didn't. Our failures are not final with God if we will repent.

Jonah's task was an unpleasant one. He had to walk through the city crying: "Yet forty days, and Nineveh shall be overthrown!" (v. 4).

It was the message of God's judgment. That has never been a pleasant message! It is regarded today as the height of arrogance and insensibility. It's not politically correct.

The fact that we so despise the message of God's judgment only means that we don't know God or ourselves. We don't realize how holy God is and how sinful we are. If we could get a true understanding of these things, we would not find the message of His judgment surprising; rather, we would find the message of His mercy surprising!

Jonah's preaching in Nineveh met with huge success. The people "believed God, proclaimed a fast, and put on sackcloth, from the greatest to the least of them" (v. 5).

A whole city turning to God! That would have been something to behold. Oh, that we could see the same today in city after city in our society!

The repenting led to relenting. The Ninevites repented and God relented—that is, God turned away from the judgment that He was planning to send against Nineveh.

This creates a problem for us. The Bible plainly affirms that the Lord never changes (Ps. 102:27; Mal. 3:6). But here we find Him changing His mind about the Ninevites. The solution to this dilemma is to keep in mind the distinction between God's character and His dealings with us. God's essential character is one of intense hatred for sin. That can't change. But it's because He can't change in that way that He does change in His dealings with us. In other words, when we turn wholeheartedly from sin, it is because of His unchangeable hatred toward sin that causes

Him to turn from His judgment.

We should let the re-sending, the repenting and the relenting of this chapter speak to us about the Lord Jesus Christ.

Unlike Jonah, Jesus didn't have to receive a second call from God the Father to undertake the work of redemption. One call was enough. The Father set the work before the Son, and He gladly and willingly took it up.

In another respect, the Lord Jesus was like Jonah. Jonah came to Nineveh preaching the forthcoming judgment of God, and Jesus also declared God's judgment. This comes as a shock to those who dreamily entertain the notion that Jesus came to this earth to only proclaim God's love. Is the problem that these folks haven't read the Gospels or rather that they have refused to believe what they read? It was Jesus who told people that they would most certainly perish if they refused to repent (Luke 13:3). It was Jesus who told His hearers to fear God because He has the power to cast into hell (Luke 12:5).

It was also Jesus who happily assured all those who repent of their sins that God will turn from His judgment. Consider His words: "Most assuredly, I say to you, he who hears My word and believes in Him who sent Me has everlasting life, and shall not come into judgment, but has passed from death into life" (John 5:24).

Have you passed from death into life?

-18-

From God's Word, the Bible...

For the wages of sin is death, but the gift of God is eternal life in Christ Jesus our Lord.

Romans 6:23

Jonah's Message and Ours

In Jonah 3 we see Jonah finally arriving in the city of Nineveh and beginning to preach. His was a bare-bones message: "Yet forty days and Nineveh shall be overthrown" (Jonah 3:1).

But folded into that message were certain brawny, muscular truths—the fact of their sin, the fact that God is holy and detests sin (Why would He judge it if that weren't the case?), and the willingness of God to forgive sin (Why would He send a prophet if that weren't the case?).

The Ninevites didn't need for Jonah to elaborate. They understood quite well that he was warning them about judgment to come because of their sins. And they understood sincere, thorough repentance was the only way for them to deal with their sin (Jonah 3:8).

The church as a whole as well as individual Christians are called today to bear witness to these truths just as Jonah was called centuries ago. We are called to proclaim the gospel. The gospel is the good news of what God has done in and through His Son, Jesus, to forgive sinners of their sins, to give them right standing with God now, and eternal glory in the future.

The gospel message assumes human sinfulness and divine judgment. It is only good news because sin and judgment are bad news. No one wants to hear bad news, but it's oftentimes necessary. A doctor doesn't withhold from a patient the unpleasant truth about his or her physical condition. The doctor's concern isn't what will make the patient happy; it's rather what is true about the patient.

Because so many in the church today seem to find Christianity's true message to be more unpleasant than unbelievers do, they make this their message: "You're okay. Now let us tell you how to live a better life."

Much of modern-day evangelism is based on the premise that people are living perfectly miserable lives, and they need to come to Christ so their lives can be improved.

The truth is that, on the one hand, there are many non-Christians who are living perfectly happy lives. What about them? Do they need Christ?

On the other hand, there are lots of Christians who have very difficult lives. I've known believers who battled illness for a good part of their lives. I've known others who constantly endured financial hardship, so much so that it was always hard for them to make ends meet.

We must be very careful about presenting the Christian message in such a way that we end up telling people that they don't need it.

The Bible's approach to evangelizing unbelievers is radically different from what has become so very common in our time. The Bible begins with our sins. The Apostle Paul writes: "For all have sinned and come short of the glory of God" (Rom. 3:23).

The Bible puts us all on equal footing. Some will always be better off in this life than others. Some will invariably have better health, more money, and more happiness than others. Some will always live in finer houses, drive nicer cars, and take more extravagant vacations.

But there's one way in which we are all alike: we're all sinners. Many object to this assertion. They often say something like this: "I know I'm not perfect, but I don't really consider myself a sinner." They use a subjective test—how they feel about themselves—to determine if they are sinners.

God, on the other hand, uses an objective test. He tells us to lay our lives alongside the Ten Commandments, keeping in mind as we do so that it's not enough to keep those commandments in a mere external fashion. For example, it's not enough to refrain from murdering someone, as the Sixth Commandment requires (Ex. 20:13). We must also refrain from hating that person (Matt. 5:21-22). Each of God's commandments testifies against us. Each one hands down the guilty verdict on us.

It's because we are all sinners that we all need Christ. Why? Because He alone has provided the way for our sins to be forgiven! He came to this earth to live without sin so He could bear our sins when He died on the cross (1 Peter 2:24).

So God's message to each of us is that we will eventually be "overthrown" if we don't turn to Christ in repentance and faith. Let's heed God's message to us as the Ninevites heeded His message to them.

-19-

From God's Word, the Bible...

Then God said to Jonah, "Is it right for you to be angry about the plant?"
And he said, "It is right for me to be angry, even to death!"
But the LORD said, "You have had pity on the plant for which you have not labored, nor made it grow, which came up in a night and perished in a night. And should I not pity Nineveh, that great city, in which are more than one hundred and twenty thousand persons who cannot discern between their right hand and their left—and much livestock?"

Jonah 4:9-11
(Read the whole passage in Jonah 4:1-11.)

The Pitiful Prophet Who Couldn't Pity

It's a pity that the book of Jonah didn't end with chapter 3. If it had only ended there we would have been left with a whole city turning to God in true repentance. We would have come away from this book with rejoicing. And we would have been spared the sight of the pitiful prophet who couldn't pity. Yes, Jonah is pitiful in chapter 4. He is a sad and pathetic figure. If the book had concluded with chapter 3, we would regard Jonah as a hero. But chapter 4 forces us to take another view of him. It causes us to shake our heads in dismay. It causes us to pity him, the pitiful prophet.

Most preachers would rejoice to see just a few converts. Jonah had a whole city of them, but he didn't rejoice. Those converts made him "exceedingly" displeased and "angry" (v. 1). They caused him to pray to the Lord, and a pitiful prayer it was! Jonah angrily accused God of being too kind, too loving, and too forgiving (v. 2). And he asked God to end his life then and there (v. 3).

So Jonah set up his little camp outside Nineveh to see what would happen to the city. He may have thought that his complaining would cause God to go back to His original plan to judge Nineveh. While Jonah waited to see (v. 5), he surely had to know what he would see. Nineveh would be spared, and it would be spared because God takes special delight in sparing repentant people.

But Jonah still had to see. So he set up a camp outside the city and waited for the forty-day period to end (Jonah 3:4).

God was already at the site Jonah picked for his camp. God had certain things prepared for His petty prophet. God always has His plans and preparations. First, there would be a "plant" to shelter Jonah from the oppressive heat (v. 6). No, there's no need to get into the business of how a plant could grow so quickly. We're talking about God, here, and God can always make special things happen.

Jonah was grateful for that plant, but, alas, it didn't last. God sent a worm to so damage the plant that it withered (v. 7). And then God sent "a vehement east wind" (v. 8). That wind, along with the brutal heat from the sun, caused Jonah to once again express the desire to die (v. 8).

I think if I had been making the decisions at this point, I would have granted Jonah's wish. But what a sight we get of God here! He continues to be kind to His exasperating prophet. He tenderly asks Jonah: "Is it right for you to be angry about the plant?" (v. 9). And, of course, Jonah blusteringly declares that he has a perfect right to be angry.

Then God dropped the hammer. Jonah pitied a mere plant, but he was angry with God for pitying people and livestock (vv. 10-11).

The book abruptly ends with a question, a question that is left hanging without Jonah's answer. It's such an abrupt ending that some might be inclined to think that we don't have the whole book of Jonah, that the last part of it got lost somewhere along the way.

I'm convinced that the question is left unanswered for another reason. God wants us to answer it for ourselves. It's as if He says to us: "It's not important for you to know how Jonah answered this question. What is important is how you answer it."

And how do we answer it? Do we have more concern for things than we do for the souls of men, women, and children?

Jonah is the pitiful prophet because he couldn't pity needy souls. Let's now look away from the sad sight of Jonah to the wonderful sight of Jesus. The Lord Jesus could never look upon people without being moved with compassion and pity (e.g., Mark 6:34). It was that heart of compassion that brought Him to this earth all the way from heaven's glory. And it was that same heart of compassion that drove Him to the cross where He died that we might live.

What was wrong with Jonah? He didn't pity Ninevites. Thank God, there's nothing wrong with Jesus. He pities sinners.

> *Come, ye sinners, poor and needy,*
> *Weak and wounded, sick and sore;*
> *Jesus ready stands to save you,*
> *Full of pity, love and pow'r.*
> (Joseph Hart)

-20-

From God's Word, the Bible...

"O Jerusalem, Jerusalem, the one who kills the prophets and stones those who are sent to her! How often I wanted to gather your children together, as a hen gathers her chicks under her wings, but you were not willing! See! Your house is left to you desolate; for I say to you, you shall see Me no more till you say, 'Blessed is He who comes in the name of the Lord!'"

Matthew 23:37-39

The Compassion of Jesus

Two men sit outside two cities. But there the similarity ends. One man sits with a heart of stone, knowing that the destruction he yearned to see would not come. Centuries later, the other man sat outside another city with a broken heart, knowing that destruction would most certainly come.

The first man, of course, was Jonah, and the city was Nineveh. The second man was Jesus, and the city was Jerusalem.

With perfect, unerring foreknowledge, the Lord Jesus could see destruction coming upon Jerusalem. And come it did in A.D. 70 at the hands of the Romans. But Jesus took no delight in the thought of judgment, which is ever God's "strange" work (Isa. 28:21, KJV). God ever delights in people turning from their sins in true repentance.

In the sorrowful words of the above passage, Jesus mentioned His desire to "gather" Jerusalem's people to Himself "as a hen gathers her chicks under her wings." But those people would have none of it. They refused to be gathered, and their refusal stirred and moved the compassionate heart of the Savior.

Matthew doesn't specifically say that Jesus wept over the city on this occasion, but, since He had done it before (Luke 19:41), it wouldn't be surprising if He wept again as He spoke these words.

The compassionate heart of Jesus—what a treasure! It was that compassionate heart that brought Him to this earth in the first place. The Apostle Paul wonderfully states: "For you know the grace of our Lord Jesus Christ, that though He was rich, yet for your sakes He became poor, that you through His poverty might become rich" (2 Cor. 8:9).

The Lord Jesus didn't have to come to this earth. He could have refused to do so, but His heart wouldn't allow Him to refuse.

Throughout His public ministry, the compassion of His heart was on display. On one occasion, the mere sight of "a great multitude" caused Him to be "moved with compassion for them because they were like sheep not having a shepherd" (Mark 6:34).

When Jesus encountered two blind men, He "had compassion and touched their eyes." And they immediately received their sight (Matt. 20:30-34).

As the Lord was entering into the city of Nain, He encountered a large group of people leaving the city to go to the cemetery. A widow had lost her son. When Jesus saw this woman, He "had compassion on her." That compassion compelled Him to raise her son from the dead (Luke 7:11-17).

It was the compassion of Jesus that later caused Him to weep outside the tomb of Lazarus before Jesus raised him from the dead (John 11:34-44).

Jesus' ministry featured many miracles—healing the sick, feeding multitudes, stilling storms, casting out demons, and, yes, raising the dead—and all of them were works of compassion.

It was Jesus' compassion that put Him on the cross. His death there was the supreme manifestation of His compassion. How great is His compassion? On the cross, He bore the wrath of God in the place of sinners.

The end of Jesus' public ministry didn't mean the end of His compassion. He ascended to the right hand of the Father in heaven, and there, as our High Priest, He sympathizes "with our weaknesses" (Heb. 4:14-15).

We must never forget that when Jesus ascended to the Father in heaven, it was in His resurrected humanity. Since He is in heaven in our humanity, it is not just that Jesus can sympathize with us in our humanity. It is rather that He cannot help but sympathize with us.

By the way, the fact that Jesus has gone into heaven in resurrected humanity is the guarantee that all who trust Him as their Lord and Savior will eventually follow Him into heaven in resurrected humanity. He is in heaven as our "forerunner" (Heb. 6:20).

When the devil suggests to us that the Lord Jesus doesn't feel sympathy and pity for us, we need to remind him that Jesus is our compassionate High Priest in heaven.

Callous Jonah and compassionate Jesus! May God help us to both appreciate the compassion of the Lord Jesus and to emulate it!

-21-

From God's Word, the Bible...

If you endure chastening, God deals with you as with sons; for what son is there whom a father does not chasten?

Now no chastening seems to be joyful for the present, but painful; nevertheless, afterward it yields the peaceable fruit of righteousness to those who have been trained by it.

Hebrews 12:7,11

Chastisement

The prophecy of Jonah confronts us with the reality of God's chastisement. To say God chastised Jonah is to say that He punished and disciplined His prophet.

Some reject out of hand the idea that God chastises. To them it is unworthy of God. It makes Him a mean, vindictive ogre who enjoys making people miserable.

But the Bible teaches otherwise. The go-to passage on the matter of God's chastisement is Hebrews 12:3-11. It first affirms that God chastises all of His children. The author indicates that we must be careful about denying the reality of God's chastisement. Such denial may mean that we don't truly have God as our Father (vv. 7-8).

The passage also shows us the reason for God's chastisement. It's not because He enjoys being unkind and harsh. It's rather due to the love that He has for all of His children. The one the Lord loves is the one that He chastens (v. 6). Yes, God has a general love for all people. We refer to that as "common grace." But God has a special love for His children, those who have come to Him in repentance of their sins and with faith in His Son, the Lord Jesus Christ. Those who enjoy that special love are those whom He chastens.

Still further, this passage reveals the intent of the chastening. It is to bring forth in us "the peaceable fruit of righteousness" (v. 11). God's chastening makes us more righteous, that is, it makes us conform more and more to the commandments of the Lord. And the more we conform to those commandments, the more peace we have!

The devil would always have us to believe that sin brings us happiness and peace, but that's a lie. Disobedience to God brings nothing but misery and woe.

As one who has had to minister to many people in their dying moments, I can tell you that I have never heard one of them express regret that he or she didn't sin more. But I've heard several express regret about not being more obedient to the Lord.

How did the Lord chastise Jonah? Let's count the ways. First, there was the tossing ship. Then there was the gulping fish. Let's not forget the gnawing worm. Finally, there was the oppressing wind.

In those four acts of chastisement, we can see the two major forms that chastisement takes. One form is the sending of adversity (the storm, the fish, and the wind). The other form is the withholding of blessing (the destruction of the vine by the worm).

We usually associate God's chastisement with adversity. If we start drifting into sinful living, and no adversity comes, we are inclined to think that God isn't chastising us. However, we need to keep the other side of the equation in mind, that is, the withholding of blessings. How much are we missing because of our disobedience? What blessings could we be enjoying if we weren't being disobedient to God?

Many churches these days are trying to cope with

shriveling attendance and declining interest. We often look at these sad realities and ask what can be done to change them. And we usually answer in terms of having more appealing programs and finding ways to "relate" to the modern generation.

Where are those who dare point out that it is possible for churches to grieve God and to experience His discipline? Where are those who suggest that the condition of the churches may very well be due to God withholding His blessings from us because we haven't been faithful in our doctrine and in our conduct? Where are those who call the church, not to better programs and promotions, but to repentance and revival?

Repentance is always the antidote for chastisement. It was when Jonah repented that the fish vomited him on to dry land. When we sin, God chastises to bring us to repentance.

The ever-active devil wages war on the teaching of chastisement. When the Lord sends it our way, the devil never hesitates to suggest that it is proof that the Lord doesn't love us. "If God loved you as much as you think, you wouldn't be going through this," the devil suggests. The proper response is to say: "Devil, I regard God's chastisement not as evidence that God doesn't love me but rather as proof that He does."

And don't forget to point the devil to the cross of Christ. That is always the greatest proof of God's love for us.

-22-

From God's Word, the Bible...

Your word is a lamp to my feet
And a light to my path.

Psalm 119:105

Where's the Mumbo? Where's the Jumbo?

Many years ago, a prominent British politician was asked if he was a Christian. He replied in this way: "I believe in the ethics of Christianity but not in the mumbo-jumbo."

How do we happen to have the term mumbo-jumbo in our vocabulary? Some think it came from a strange ritual that African husbands used to frighten disobedient, rebellious wives into submission. Others suggest that it refers to a grotesque idol that was worshiped by certain African tribes.

This much is clear: at its root, mumbo-jumbo refers to superstitious, meaningless rituals that obscure and create confusion.

If mumbo-jumbo is designed to obscure or create confusion, we must surely say that politicians specialize in it. And here is a politician criticizing Christianity for it! What an amazing and rich irony!

So what about Christianity? Is it mumbo-jumbo, as the politician suggested? Is it based on superstition or on fact? Does it consist of meaningless rituals? Is it confusing?

Here is the central tenet of Christianity—God sent His Son into this world to save sinners (Matt. 1:21; Luke 19:10; 1 Tim. 1:15).

That certainly seems clear enough to me. Where is the mumbo? Where is the jumbo?

It certainly isn't mere superstition to believe that we are sinners. The fact of sin is written large before our eyes every single day of our lives. We see it all around us, and, if we care to admit it, we see it in ourselves. The very fact that the politician to whom I've been referring would applaud Christian ethics tells us that he was indirectly admitting the fact of sin. There would be no need for ethics if it weren't for sin. By the way, this politician lived through the two world wars that put the reality of sin in graphic display and focus.

Is it mere superstition to believe that Jesus actually lived? The mumbo-jumbo politician wasn't denying the existence of Jesus. He knew better than that! Only a handful of people are silly enough to believe that Jesus never lived.

Is it mere superstition to say Jesus came from heaven? The prophecies He fulfilled, the miracles He performed, the words that He spoke, the lives that He changed—and, most of all, the grave that He conquered—unite to say Jesus was from heaven.

And what about Jesus' death on the cross? Is that mumbo-jumbo? The Bible says otherwise. It isn't silly superstition to believe that Jesus was crucified, and it isn't baseless superstition to believe that His was a special death, a death designed to accomplish something special, namely, forgiveness for sinners. How are we to respond to those who think the cross of Christ is mere superstition? Let's point them to the countless millions who have found, in that cross, relief from the guilt of their sins, and release from the fear of judgment to come.

And what about baptism and the Lord's Supper? Are they nothing more than confusing, superstitious rituals? The former, baptism, is the way we publicly profess our faith in Christ and identify ourselves with Him. And the Lord's Supper is the public celebration and commemoration of the saving work of Jesus on our behalf. Superstitious and confusing rituals? They make perfect sense to me!

I'm inclined to think that many who reject Christianity do so not because there is no evidence for it but because they don't like where the evidence leads. And I'm inclined to think that those who think Christianity is confusing may, in fact, find it to be too plain about their sins and about judgment to come. They reject it because they fancy themselves to be very intelligent, and salvation provided by a man dying on a cross seems absurd to them.

If Christianity is mumbo-jumbo, I have this to say: Blessed mumbo-jumbo! It gives me the assurance that my sins are forgiven and that I have a home in heaven through Christ. So I want my cup filled with it. Let me drink it dry, and then please fill it again and again!

And what about the politician who dismissed Christianity as mumbo-jumbo? He died many years ago. So now he knows the truth of the matter. If we don't know the truth of Christianity now, death will finally make it clear to us.

-23-

From God's Word, the Bible...

But you must continue in the things which you have learned and been assured of, knowing from whom you have learned them, and that from childhood you have known the Holy Scriptures, which are able to make you wise for salvation through faith which is in Christ Jesus.

2 Timothy 3:14-15

The Man Who Got His Bible Back

A young medical student was strapped for cash. So he sold his Bible for a small amount. It was the Bible that his mother had given him. She had written his name on its flyleaf. Let that soak in! A young man sold his Bible for a small amount! Yes, he was in need of money, but the small amount he received for his Bible wouldn't have made any real difference in his financial situation. It's apparent that he didn't really value the Bible. I'm not talking about a dollars-and-cents value but rather about the value of its message, which is the Lord Jesus Christ and the saving mission that brought Him to this earth. The person who understands the treasure that the Bible is might give it away to someone who needs it, but it's unlikely that he will sell it. If he does, he will quickly replace it with another.

But let's get back to the young medical student. He went on to complete his training and began his career. One day a seriously injured man was brought to the hospital. His injuries were so severe that nothing could be done to save him. He told the doctor that he had no relatives but that he would like for his landlady to come and bring him "the book."

"What book?" the doctor asked.

"She will know," was the reply.

The man only lived a few days, but the doctor noticed on his daily visits that he was always calm, peaceful, and smiling.

When it came time to dispose of his few possessions, a nurse held up a book and asked: "What shall we do with this?" What kind of book is it?" asked the doctor.

"It's the Bible," the nurse replied.

The doctor looked at the Bible, and, to his utter astonishment, it was the very Bible that he had sold so many years before. His name, in his dear mother's handwriting, was still there.

As he stood gazing upon his old Bible, the doctor thought about the peace that the dying man had enjoyed in his last days. He was sure that peace came from the very Bible that he had sold long ago for what he would call "a ridiculous price."

So the doctor kept the Bible. He got it back, but he also got something that he had never possessed before. He read the Bible's message of salvation and received the Lord Jesus Christ as his Savior.

That doctor was W.P. Mackay of Scotland. He is probably best known to us as the author of these words:

> *We praise Thee, O God, For the Son of Thy love;*
> *For Jesus, who died, And is now gone above.*

> *We praise Thee, O God, For Thy Spirit of light,*
> *Who has shown us our Savior, And scattered our night.*

> *All glory and praise, To the Lamb that was slain,*
> *Who has borne all our sins, And hath cleansed every stain.*

This is a hymn about the salvation that Mackay came to understand and to receive. It is the salvation provided by Christ "who died and is now gone above." It is the salvation that came to us as a result of the Spirit of God enlightening us. He is the "Spirit of light" who showed us the Savior and "scattered our night." It is the salvation that was purchased for us when Jesus died on the cross a sin-bearing death. He bore "all our sins" and "hath cleansed every stain."

But Mackay's hymn is also about something else. It's about God's people losing sight of the wonder and glory of their salvation and allowing themselves to become cold and indifferent. So Mackay's fourth verse and chorus read:

> *Revive us again; Fill each heart with Thy love;*
> *May each soul be rekindled, With fire from above.*

> *Hallelujah! Thine the glory! Hallelujah! Amen!*
> *Hallelujah! Thine the glory! Revive us again.*

Mackay's hymn, *Revive Us Again*, has a mystery running through it. On one hand, it celebrates the glory of salvation. On the other hand, it recognizes the need for revival. With such a glorious salvation, how is it that we ever need revival? But we often do. How can we continue to feel awe about salvation and continue to be warmly devoted to the Lord? Perhaps we need to get our Bibles back.

-24-

From God's Word, the Bible...

For to me, to live is Christ, and to die is gain. But if I live on in the flesh, this will mean fruit from my labor; yet what I shall choose I cannot tell. For I am hard-pressed between the two, having a desire to depart and be with Christ, which is far better.

Philippians 1:21-23

A Hymn's Question Answered

It was late on the evening of September 21, 1921, and hymn-writer William J. Kirkpatrick was still working at his desk. After she had been sleeping for a while, his wife noticed that the light in his study was still on. "Don't you think you had better come to bed?" she called. He responded: "I'm all right, dear, I have a little work I want to finish. Go back to sleep, everything is all right."

She went back to sleep and once again awoke to see his light still on. This time he didn't answer her call. She went to the study to find his lifeless body still sitting in his chair and slumped over his desk.

The poem on which he had been working read:

> *Just as Thou wilt, Lord, this is my cry,*
> *Just as Thou wilt, to live or die.*
> *I am Thy servant, Thou knowest best,*
> *Just as Thou wilt, Lord, labor or rest.*

> *Just as Thou wilt, Lord, which shall it be?*
> *Life everlasting waiting for me –*
> *Or shall I tarry, here at Thy feet?*
> *Just as Thou wilt, Lord, whatever is meet.*

Kirkpatrick had asked: "Lord, which shall it be?" And the Lord had answered. It was not to be more life on this earth. It was to be death. But in answering with death for Kirkpatrick, the Lord was not shortchanging him or mistreating him. He was doing the best possible thing for His servant, receiving him into His presence where he would know nothing but perfect peace and joy.

We who believe Christ can allow ourselves to love life in this world so much that we give the impression that death is the ultimate disaster. We can begin to regard life in heaven as second best to life in this world. But heaven is always best, and death is never a disaster for the child of God.

Many centuries before Kirkpatrick entered this world, the Apostle Paul essentially asked the Lord the same question: "Which shall it be, Lord, life or death?"

The apostle felt torn. On one hand, he had a desire to remain on this earth for a while so he could continue to labor for the Lord. On the other hand, he had an intense desire "to depart and be with Christ," which he described as being "far better."

It was always Christ with the Apostle Paul. To live was to serve Christ. To die was to be with Christ. With those two possibilities, there was no way that Paul could lose.

The most important question anyone can ask is this: "Am I sure that I'm going to heaven?"

I'm convinced that the major thing that keeps people from asking themselves that question is the belief that nothing has to be done to enter heaven. But there is something that has to be done. We have to repent of our sins and trust in the Lord Jesus Christ. He is the way to heaven, and there is no other way (John 14:6; Acts 4:12). He came from heaven to make the way for sinners to go to heaven.

I'm certainly not in the category of the Apostle Paul, or, for that matter, William J. Kirkpatrick. But I can say that I am looking forward to heaven. This world has given me my fill of tears and heartaches. What a blessed thing it will be to live in a land where there is no crying, no pain, no sorrow, and no death!

All of God's people will eventually receive the Lord's call to enter heaven, even as William Kirkpatrick did. But now we wait, and while we wait, we sing:

> *There's a land that is fairer than day,*
> *And by faith we can see it afar;*
> *For the Father waits over the way*
> *To prepare us a dwelling place there.*
>
> *In the sweet by and by,*
> *We shall meet on that beautiful shore;*
> *In the sweet by and by,*
> *We shall meet on that beautiful shore.*
>
> *We shall sing on that beautiful shore*
> *The melodious songs of the blessed;*
> *And our spirits shall sorrow no more,*
> *Not a sigh for the blessing of rest.*
> (Sanford Fillmore Bennett)

It will be a joy to land on "that beautiful shore" and to see the Apostle Paul and William J. Kirkpatrick. But the best sight of heaven will be the Lord Jesus Christ, and the best sight of Christ will be His nail-pierced hands.

-25-

From God's Word, the Bible...

Then they spat in His face and beat Him; and others struck Him with the palms of their hands, saying, "Prophesy to us, Christ! Who is the one who struck You?"

Likewise the chief priests also, mocking with the scribes and elders, said, "He saved others; Himself He cannot save. If He is the King of Israel, let Him now come down from the cross, and we will believe Him. He trusted in God; let Him deliver Him now if He will have Him; for He said, 'I am the Son of God.'"

Matthew 26:67-68; Matthew 27:41-43

The Message of Heaven in the Mockery of Hell

Mockery was a major part of what Jesus had to endure the last hours of His life. Matthew records five distinct episodes of the mockery heaped upon Him. Two of those episodes occurred before Jesus was nailed to the cross. They were that of the religious leaders after they sentenced Him (Matt. 26:67-68) and that of the soldiers as they prepared Him for crucifixion (27:27-31). The other three episodes occurred while Jesus was on the cross. These instances of mockery came from some who passed by (27:39-40), the religious leaders (27:41-43), and from the two thieves crucified alongside Jesus (27:44).

So two of the five instances of men mocking Jesus came from the religious leaders. I want us to think about those two instances. More specifically, I want us to look for the message of heaven in their mockery.

I'm calling the mockery of the religious leaders the mockery of hell because it was driven and inspired by the devil himself. How do we know this? First, it was the mockery of hardness, and hardness comes from hell.

The hardness of their mockery is easy to see. They had just sentenced a man to die. In his splendid little book, *The Cross He Bore*, Frederick Leahy writes:

> To sentence someone to death is an awesome responsibility. One does not expect that judges who have passed such a sentence will almost immediately turn to revelry or frivolity. They should be burdened men. A solemn silence should pervade the courtroom. There should be a profound awareness of the majesty of the law.[1]

But these men were so hardened in their sinfulness that they couldn't feel the awesome weight of the sentence they had just pronounced.

Theirs was also the mockery of hell because of its blindness. These leaders were blinded in regard to the true identity of the man before them. Little did they know that they were mocking, not just a king, but the King of kings and the Lord of lords. They were mocking the very One who had given them life and the very One who at that moment was giving them the breath they needed to express their vicious insults and the strength they needed to deliver their crushing blows.

How were they supposed to know who Jesus was? He had stacked proof on top of proof in the many miracles that He had performed. But these men couldn't see the truth

---

[1] Frederick S. Leahy, *The Cross He Bore*, The Banner of Truth Trust, Edinburgh, Scotland, 1996, p.43

about Jesus. They were blind to it, and blindness to the truth about Him comes right out of hell (2 Cor. 4:4).

Theirs was also the mockery of hatred. These men didn't merely disagree with Jesus. They hated Him with a fierce hatred. Why did they hate Him so intensely? He had claimed to be their Messiah, but He wasn't the kind of Messiah that they wanted. They wanted a temporal Messiah who would break their bondage to the Roman government and lead Israel to great glory.

They thought their hatred for Jesus was well founded and justified, but hatred for Christ is always hell-fueled and hell-driven.

As we've noticed, there were two instances of the religious leaders mocking Jesus. One was immediately after they sentenced Him. The other was while He was on the cross. As they stood at the foot of the cross, they cried: "He saved others; Himself He cannot save" (Matt. 27:42).

In their hardness and their blindness, these men didn't realize that they were actually telling the truth about Jesus. They were, in fact, declaring the very message of heaven. There at the foot of the cross, these men became preachers of the gospel of Christ. No, they didn't realize it then, and most of them probably never realized it. But their lack of understanding doesn't change the fact that it was the message of heaven they declared.

Jesus came to this earth to provide redemption for all who will believe in Him. To do that, He had to die a special death on the cross. It was special because He actually received the wrath of God in the place of sinners. If Jesus had come down from the cross to save Himself, the plan of redemption would have failed. He could not simultaneously save Himself from the cross and save sinners.

So in the mockery of hell heaped on Jesus, we hear the message of heaven. And the joke is on the devil.

-26-

From God's Word, the Bible...

Then, as they were afraid and bowed their faces to the earth, they said to them, "Why do you seek the living among the dead? He is not here, but is risen! Remember how He spoke to you when He was still in Galilee..."

Luke 24:5-6

Easter: Amazing, But Not Surprising

Easter is, as one hymn writer put it, "Our triumphant, holy day." Every Christian loves Easter. Easter thrills Christians.

But I have to say that while Easter thrills me, it doesn't surprise me. To the contrary, I would be surprised if there had been no Easter.

Now, Christmas and Good Friday surprise me. Immensely so! Christmas was born in the heart of God centuries before Jesus was born. Before the world began, God looked down the long corridor of time and saw that the man He intended to create would fall into sin and bring disastrous consequences upon the entire human race. So Christmas was born. God looked at the forthcoming human sin in all of its nastiness and filthiness and decided that He would send His Son into the midst of it all. He would send His Son into this world as one of us. His Son would take our humanity even to the point of actually being born of a woman and coming into this world as a tiny baby.

The Father set this plan before the Son there in eternity past. And the Son agreed! He didn't have to agree. The Son of God could have said: "I am not going to humiliate Myself for sinners who have trampled My Father's commands and spit in His face." And the Son wouldn't have done wrong if He had refused to come. He could have left us to ourselves in the sin and misery that we brought upon ourselves, and He Himself would still have been pure and holy.

But what is this? He agrees to come! He agrees there when the Father first set the plan before Him, and as human history begins and the centuries begin to come and go, He, the Son, still agrees.

Finally, the time arrives. The date that God the Father circled on the calendar back there in eternity past finally comes. And God the Son does just as He agreed to do. He steps into human history as a baby. Now we have a marvel that can't be measured or described. The infinite God is in a tiny package. God is in that baby born in Bethlehem. It would have been amazing to me had the Lord agreed to come to this earth as a full-grown man, but He comes as a baby! Charles Wesley attempts to describe this marvel in these words:

> *Our God contracted to a span,*
> *Incomprehensibly made man.*

We will never appreciate the fact that Jesus came until we appreciate the fact that He didn't have to come.

Christmas is stunning to me. And so is Good Friday. It tells me that this One who didn't have to come went to a cross and died.

Just as He didn't have to come, so He didn't have to die.

He could have spoken a mere word and instantly slaughtered those who wanted to nail Him to the cross. Or after they nailed Him there, He could have stepped down in a blaze of glory. He didn't need the angels of heaven to assist Him, but He could have called them (Matt. 26:53). And one wonders if those very angels didn't surround Calvary with bated breath as they expected His command.

But He didn't step down from the cross, and He didn't call for the angels. He stayed on the cross to die, and die He did, crying in His last moments: "It is finished!" (John 19:30).

A man dying! What's so unusual about that? In this case, it was a man dying a death that He didn't have to die to achieve something for people who didn't deserve it. On the cross, Jesus received the wrath of God that we deserve so we don't have to experience that wrath if we will receive for ourselves what He did there. Once again, we look to Charles Wesley:

> *'Tis myst'ry all: th' Immortal dies:*
> *Who can explore His strange design?*
> *In vain the firstborn seraph tries*
> *To sound the depths of love divine.*
> *'Tis mercy all! Let earth adore,*
> *Let angel minds inquire no more.*

God takes our humanity and dies! Christmas? Amazing! Good Friday? Absolutely astonishing!

And now Easter comes to tell us that this One who came at Christmas and died on Good Friday has risen from the grave. And I have to say: "Of course, He did. How could it be otherwise?"

-27-

From God's Word, the Bible...

Be merciful to me, O God, be merciful to me!
For my soul trusts in You;
And in the shadow of Your wings I will make my refuge,
Until these calamities have passed by.

I will cry out to God Most High,
To God who performs all things for me.

Psalm 57:1-2

A Psalm for Cave Dwellers

David wrote this psalm from a cave. Why was he, the hero who had slain Goliath, dwelling in a cave? He was hiding from King Saul, who hated him and wanted to kill him.

David wouldn't have been in this cave if he hadn't been in trouble. We can call it "the cave of David's trouble."

If David's cave represents trouble, we have to say we're all cave dwellers from time to time. It's possible to live in a comfortable house and still be a cave dweller.

What does David the cave dweller have to say to all the rest of us cave dwellers?

First, he shows us that *the cave of our trouble can and should be the cave of our refuge.* From the cave of his trouble, David cries to God:

> *And in the shadow of Your wings I will make my refuge*
> *Until these calamities have passed by* (v. 1).

The picture here is of the little chick that runs to its mother to take refuge under her wings. David's circumstances were such that he felt as helpless and frightened as that chick. As the chick was confident that his mother would protect him, so David was confident that God would protect him. We know, of course, that the hen can't protect her chicks from every conceivable danger. But God is sufficient for us in every trial and every circumstance.

David also shows us that *the cave of our trouble can and should be the cave of our prayer.*

Prayer is the way in which David took refuge in God. This whole 57th Psalm is a prayer. It shows us that:

- we should pray when we are in trouble;
- we can and should speak honestly to God;
- we must pray sincerely from our hearts;
- we must pray with a consciousness of the greatness of God.

David also encourages us to believe that *the cave of our trouble is the cave of God's purpose for us.* He tells us that God "performs all things" for him (v. 2).

So David wasn't in this cave by accident. His presence there didn't catch God off guard or take Him by surprise. That cave was part of God's purpose for him. It was necessary to make him into the man that God wanted him to be, the man who could serve as king over Israel and write psalms such as this one.

We're inclined to take our difficult circumstances to mean that God has forsaken us or that He doesn't care for us. We must learn to look at those circumstances as proofs that He hasn't forsaken us, and He does care for us.

A marvelous day of explanation is coming for every one of God's people. God will finally explain what His purpose was in sending various hardships our way. When He explains, we will see the whole picture, and we will be amazed at what He accomplished with us through our trials.

Yet another lesson that David offers us is this: *the cave of our trouble can and should be the cave of our opportunity.*

Every trial that comes our way gives us the opportunity to examine our hearts and to say with David:

My heart is steadfast, O God, my heart is steadfast (v. 7).

And every trial gives us the opportunity to confess our faith in God and to offer praise to Him, as David did (vv. 9-11).

Finally, David shows us that *the cave of our trouble will not always be the cave of our trouble.* David knew that his own "calamities" would pass by (v. 1).

Our calamities will pass by as well. We see many of them pass by in this life. Things come and trouble us for a while, and then they are gone. When this happens, we must not forget to thank God for His goodness to us. How quick we are to complain when trouble comes! How slow we can be to thank God when the trouble passes!

The fact that some calamities don't pass by in this life doesn't mean that they will never pass. Our troubles aren't eternal. A day is coming when every single trouble will pass by for the children of God. And that will all be due to the saving work of Jesus Christ.

The only calamity that never passes is the one that applies to those who don't receive Christ (John 3:36). Have you turned away from sin and are you trusting in Him?

-28-

From God's Word, the Bible...

... but supposing Him to have been in the company, they went a day's journey, and sought Him among their relatives and acquaintances.

Jesus said to her, "Woman, why are you weeping? Whom are you seeking?" She, supposing Him to be the gardener, said to Him, "Sir, if You have carried Him away, tell me where You have laid Him, and I will take Him away."

Luke 2:44; John 20:15

Mistaken Assumptions

Two occasions, two assumptions, two mistakes—that's the story of these two verses of Scripture.

On the first occasion, we have the mistake of assuming Jesus to be present when He was actually absent.

On the second occasion, we have the mistake of assuming Jesus to be absent when He was actually present.

The first mistaken assumption was that of Joseph and Mary. Having gone to Jerusalem to attend the Feast of the Passover, they were on their way back to Nazareth. It was common in those days for pilgrims to Jerusalem to travel in companies or caravans. Joseph and Mary were in their caravan and a day's journey from Jerusalem. They assumed that Jesus was "in the company," but He wasn't. He had "lingered behind in Jerusalem" (Luke 2:43).

It was back to Jerusalem for Joseph and Mary when they realized their error. There they found Jesus in the temple engaged in dialogue with "the teachers" (v. 46), who were

~ 125 ~

"astonished at His understanding and answers" (v. 47).

Joseph and Mary had wrongly assumed that Jesus was present when He was absent. I wonder how often their error has been repeated through the centuries. I wonder how frequently it is being repeated in our time.

It's so very easy for us to assume that the Lord is present in our church services when He has actually withdrawn. The church can be very much like Samson of old "who did not know that the LORD had departed from him" (Judg. 16:20).

But isn't the Lord always with His people? Yes, there is a sense in which He is. But we might say He can be present and absent at the same time. He can be present but withdrawn. He can be present, but not present to bless. His can be a grieved presence. We can think of it in terms of a husband and wife being present in their home but so alienated from each other that they are in fact absent from each other.

What causes the Lord to be so grieved with His churches that He withdraws from them? He's surely grieved when we distort and misrepresent His truth to make it fit modern beliefs and assumptions. He must surely be driven away by irreverent and silly shenanigans that make the church seem more like a carnival than a church. He's offended when we go through the motions of worship while our hearts are far from Him. He's most certainly vexed when His people live without regard to His commandments. Nothing is sadder than for God's people to assure themselves that the Lord is with them when He's not even on the premises.

The urgent need of this hour is for God's people to cry to Him to "come down," or, should we say, "come back?" (Isa. 64:1).

Now we come to the mistaken assumption of Mary Magdalene on the day of Jesus' resurrection. With the risen Christ standing right there before her, Mary Magdalene supposed Him "to be the gardener."

Jesus was present, but she assumed that He was absent. Even though Jesus had promised that He would rise from the grave, Mary Magdalene was not expecting it. She was lacking in faith.

We can do the same as she. We can look at the increasing evil of the world and the steadily growing hatred for Christianity as proofs that the Lord has completely withdrawn from us and left us to fend for ourselves. The Lord calls us to believe that while He doesn't approve of the evil all around us, He is working through it to bring all things to this end: every knee bowing before King Jesus, and every tongue confessing that He is Lord! (Phil. 2:9-11).

Satan would also have us look at our trials and hardships as indications that God is absent from us. But Scripture affirms that the very hardships that seem to indicate God's absence prove His presence. God is always at work in the lives of His people to conform them to the image of Christ. To achieve that end, He employs different methods. When He chooses to send difficulties our way, it doesn't mean that He has abandoned His purpose for us. It rather means that He is advancing that purpose through those very difficulties.

Assuming Christ to be present when He is absent will keep us from truly seeking Him. Assuming Christ to be absent when He is present will keep us from enjoying Him. So let's check our assumptions.

-29-

From God's Word, the Bible...

"Therefore do not worry, saying, 'What shall we eat?' or 'What shall we drink?' or 'What shall we wear?' For after all these things the Gentiles seek. For your heavenly Father knows that you need all these things."

Matthew 6:31-32

My Heavenly Father Watches Over Me

To say William Clark Martin was a hymn writer is a gigantic understatement. He wrote hundreds and hundreds of hymns. We know little about William Martin. He was born on Christmas Day in 1864, and he died on August 30, 1914. He served as a pastor of Baptist churches in Connecticut, Massachusetts, Indiana, and Florida.

Some of his hymns have unusual titles: *Although Satan is Busy, I Get Along Quite Easy*, *Be a Sunny, Sunny Christian*, *Do Not Draw the Curtains over the Windows of the Soul*, and *I Cannot Explain It for Grace is So Strange*.

The best known of Martin's hymns is *My Heav'nly Father Watches Over Me*.

> *I trust in God wherever I may be,*
> *Upon the land, or on the rolling sea,*
> *For come what may, from day to day,*
> *My heav'nly Father watches over me.*

Refrain

I trust in God, I know He cares for me;
On mountain bleak or on the stormy sea;
Though billows roll, He keeps my soul;
My heav'nly Father watches over me.

He makes the rose an object of His care,
He guides the eagle through the pathless air,
And surely He remembers me;
My heav'nly Father watches over me.

I trust in God, for, in the lions' den,
On battlefield, or in the prison pen,
Through praise or blame, through flood or flame,
My heav'nly Father watches over me.

The valley may be dark, the shadows deep,
But, oh, the Shepherd guards His lonely sheep;
And through the gloom He'll lead me home,
My heav'nly Father watches over me.

It's easy to see why this hymn has been a favorite of God's people through the years. It calls us away from that thing which is easy for us to do—worrying—to embrace that thing which we often find so hard to do—trusting God.

This is a hymn of many extremes. It takes us from the land to the sea and from the lions' den to the battlefield and the prison pen. It takes us from the "mountain bleak" to the valley, which is "dark" with "shadows deep."

The common denominator in these various figures is hardship or difficulty. As he journeys through this world, the Christian often finds the mountain to be "bleak," the sea to be "stormy," and the valley to be "dark."

We can be thankful that while difficulty is often the case,

it's not always the case. Every Christian has his share of bright days and calm seas. But there is something that is always the case—and that is the care of our heavenly Father. He knows each of us, just as He knows each rose and makes each one "an object of His care." He knows each eagle that soars through the air, and He guides each one through "the pathless air."

Any Christian who thinks that he or she is too small or insignificant to be noticed and known by God is simply wrong.

I like Martin's hymn very much. I need it. I need to be reminded that I'm always the object of my heavenly Father's care. I need to be reminded that I can trust Him in all of the variables of life.

But I have to say that I would like Martin's hymn even better if he had written a verse about why we must believe that our heavenly Father cares for us. So I hope he won't mind if I add this verse to his splendid hymn:

> *I trust in God, I know He cares for me;*
> *He proved it beyond dispute on Calvary.*
> *His Son took sin's blow, so I can know;*
> *My heavn'ly Father watches over me.*

-30-

From God's Word, the Bible...

These things I have written to you who believe in the name of the Son of God, that you may know that you have eternal life, and that you may continue to believe in the name of the Son of God.

1 John 5:13

Blessed Assurance

Christians love to sing Fanny Crosby's hymn *Blessed Assurance*, but many would probably admit that they lack the very assurance that they sing about. In my years as a pastor, people often came to me with this lament: "I'm not sure that I've been saved."

There are three possibilities on this matter of assurance—assured and not saved, saved and not assured, and both saved and assured.

In the above verse, the Apostle John expressed the desire for his readers to be in the third category. He wanted them to be saved and assured that they were saved. To that end, John counseled them to ask themselves these questions:

- Are they keeping the Lord's commandments?
- Are they confessing the truth about the Lord Jesus?
- Are they demonstrating love toward their brothers and sisters in Christ?

It's interesting that John mentioned each of these three

tests three times in his short epistle. We find the commandment test in 2:3-6; 2:8-3:10; 4:13-21, the confession test in 2:18-27; 4:1-6, 13-21, and the love test in 2:7-11; 3:11-18; 4:7-12.

The commandment test can be particularly challenging for us. The reason is that we know how frequently we fail to live as we should. The commandment test seems to suggest that we should be free from sin, and we know that we aren't.

The love test can also prove to be very challenging. We sometimes find it hard to love some of our Christian family. Someone put it in these memorable words:

> *To live above with the saints we love,*
> *That will be glory;*
> *But to live below with the saints we know,*
> *That's a different story.*

We will always be in trouble if we think John is requiring perfection of us. That is, in fact, what many unbelievers seem to require. They think Christians claim to be perfect, and they can be very eager to dismiss Christianity as meaningless when they see any sin in a Christian.

But Christians aren't perfect in this world, and the apostle himself admits that in no uncertain terms: "If we say that we have no sin, we deceive ourselves, and the truth is not in us" (1:8).

Do Christians fail? Yes. But these things are also true of believers:

- They agree that the commandments of God are good and right.
- They know that they should obey them, and they strive to do so.
- They are grieved when they fail, and they repent.

Christians don't enjoy sin. It makes them miserable. Unbelievers are comfortable in sin, but Christians aren't. While hogs enjoy wallowing in the mud, sheep don't.

Some Christians say that they never lack assurance of their salvation because they have the witness of the Spirit. They remind us of these words from the Apostle Paul: "The Spirit Himself bears witness with our spirit that we are children of God...." (Rom. 8:16).

We certainly don't want to deny that there is such a thing as the witness of the Spirit! But we must also not use that precious witness to exempt ourselves from the evidences given by the Apostle John. In other words, we must never say that we don't need to keep the commandments of the Lord or love our brothers and sisters in Christ because we have the witness of the Spirit. The witness of the Spirit is in tandem with these evidences and not in isolation from them.

The most helpful thing to me on this matter of assurance comes by looking to the Lord Jesus Christ. He is not only my Savior. He is my assurance. The devil wants to shift our focus from the Savior to our experience of salvation. He will tell us that we should have felt this and we should have said that when we received the Lord. The fact that we didn't feel as we should have and didn't say what we should have mean we're not saved. So argues Satan. But our assurance doesn't rest on us having a certain kind of salvation experience. It rests rather on Christ. We may not have had a perfect experience, but He died on the cross. When Satan seeks to shift our focus from Christ to ourselves, we must always shift it back to Christ, saying with Fanny Crosby:

Blessed assurance, Jesus is mine!
Oh, what a foretaste of glory divine!

-31-

From God's Word, the Bible...

Finally, my brethren, be strong in the Lord and in the power of His might. Put on the whole armor of God, that you may be able to stand against the wiles of the devil.

Ephesians 6:10-11

Liar and Truth-Teller

The acronym is LIAR. It is the *Lexicon of Intentionally Ambiguous Recommendations*. For someone who has proven himself to be a lazy employee, one might recommend him to another business by saying: "You would be very fortunate to get this person to work for you." For an employee who has been habitually in trouble with the law, one could say: "He is a man of many convictions." For an employee who is lacking in qualifications, one could write: "I most enthusiastically recommend this candidate with no qualifications whatsoever." Or one might say: "All in all, I cannot say enough good things about this candidate or recommend him too highly."

What about the employee who is so poor that the company would be better off to leave the position vacant? Here's the "recommendation" for that: "I can assure you that no person would be better for the job."

For a former employee who couldn't get along with his fellow-employees, one might say: "I am pleased to say that this candidate is a former colleague of mine."

And here is the "recommendation" for the person who deserves no consideration at all: "I would urge you to waste no time in making this person an offer of employment."

In this lexicon, the term "intentionally ambiguous" is the delicate, sanitary name for deception, and while we might find these "recommendations" to be clever and funny, we wouldn't enjoy being on the receiving end of them.

Deception has been going on for a very long time. It is almost as old as the human race itself. Satan was the original practitioner of it in the Garden of Eden, and he continues to use it with great success. He is the master deceiver.

One of Satan's favorite ways to practice deception is by putting ministers into pulpits who distort the message of Christianity. The Apostle Paul put it in these words: ". . . Satan himself transforms himself into an angel of light. Therefore it is no great thing if his ministers also transform themselves into ministers of righteousness, whose end will be according to their works" (2 Cor. 11:14b-15).

Satan uses his false ministers to lull people to sleep in regard to spiritual matters. He uses them to say that we are basically good and that we need not worry about the matter of sin. He uses them to persuade us that if there is such a thing as sin, it isn't serious because there is no judgment to come. He uses them to convince us that all are headed for heaven and, therefore, don't need the Lord Jesus as our Savior.

The thing the Bible always stresses about the devil is his subtlety. He doesn't come to us in a frightful way. Paul says he "transforms himself into an angel of light." His ministers don't come across as uncouth, crude clodhoppers. They are smooth, suave, sophisticated, clever, and funny. They are so personally appealing that naïve listeners assume that they couldn't possibly be wrong. But wrong they are, as those who heed them will eventually learn.

On the other hand, the Lord Jesus is the supreme truth-teller. He told the truth about the devil when He said: ". . .he does not stand in the truth, because there is no truth in him. When he speaks a lie, he speaks from his own resources, for he is a liar and the father of it" (John 8:44).

He also plainly warned about the devil's ministers: "Beware of false prophets, who come to you in sheep's clothing, but inwardly they are ravenous wolves" (Matt. 7:15).

He also tells us the truth about ourselves. He confronts us with the reality of our sinfulness (John 3:19-20) and with the certainty of divine judgment (Matt. 25:31-46).

Still further, He tells us the truth about Himself, affirming for us that He came from God (John 8:42) to provide salvation for sinners, and that we will have that salvation if we repent of our sins (Luke 13:5) and trust in Him (John 3:16,18).

The Bible is not "intentionally ambiguous" about Satan or the Lord Jesus. It is intentionally unambiguous about both, and it calls us to be intentionally unambiguous about them as well by rejecting the devil and his schemes and by receiving Christ and His salvation.

About the Author

Roger Ellsworth is a retired pastor, active in ministry and writing, who lives in Jackson, Tennessee. He and his wife, Sylvia, love the message of the Bible, and they enjoy sharing the wonderful counsel of the Word of God in language that ordinary people can understand and appreciate.

Roger has written numerous books on the Christian faith, and has exercised a preaching ministry for over fifty years. His sermons are available to listen for free on SermonAudio.com.

The Series

Enjoy collecting the My Coffee Cup Meditations Series.

A Dog and A Clock 978-0-9988812-9-4 (Series#1)
The "Thumbs-Up" Man 978-0-9988812-5-6 (Series#2)
When God Blocks Our Path 978-0-9988812-4-9 (Series#3)
Fading Lines, Unfading Hope 978-0-9996559-1-7 (Series#4)
The Day the Milk Spilled 978-0-9965168-6-0 (Series#5)
"Where Are the Donuts?" 978-0-9965168-7-7 (Series#6)
Sure Signs of Heavenly Hope 978-0-9988812-1-8 (Series#7)
My Dog Knows It's Sunday 978-0-9996559-6-2 (Series#8)
Rover and the Cows 978-0-9996559-7-9 (Series#9)
Apples of Gold in Settings of Silver (Series#10)
Old Houses, New Houses (Series#11)
The Gold Key on the Silver Thread (Series#12)

Collect All the Books!

www.mycoffeecupmeditations.com